LIFE IN
STRANGEWAYS

LIFE IN STRANGEWAYS

FROM RIOTS TO REDEMPTION, MY THIRTY-TWO YEARS BEHIND BARS

ALAN LORD
WITH **ANITA ARMSTRONG**

JOHN BLAKE

Published by John Blake Publishing Ltd,
3 Bramber Court, 2 Bramber Road,
London W14 9PB, England

www.johnblakepublishing.co.uk

www.facebook.com/johnblakebooks [f]
twitter.com/jblakebooks [t]

This edition published in 2015

ISBN: 978 1 78418 601 2

British Library Cataloguing-in-Publication Data:

A catalogue record for this book is available from the British Library.

Design by www.envydesign.co.uk

Printed in Great Britain by CPI Group (UK) Ltd

3 5 7 9 10 8 6 4

Papers used by John Blake Publishing are natural, recyclable products made
from wood grown in sustainable forests. The manufacturing processes
conform to the environmental regulations of the country of origin.

Every attempt has been made to contact the relevant copyright-holders,
but some were unobtainable. We would be grateful if the
appropriate people could contact us.

ABOUT THE AUTHOR

Alan Lord was born on 30 May 1961 at St Mary's Hospital in Manchester. His father was from Belize, Central America, and his mother was Anglo-Irish. Alan has one sister, Eunice, who was born in 1959 and is now recovering from cancer. Both of their parents passed away while Alan was serving a life sentence in prison. Alan was informed of his father's dying wish to see his son, but his request was rejected by the prison authorities.

ACKNOWLEDGEMENTS

To Anita Armstrong (writer): for believing in me, for her hard work and determination, for understanding me, and for all her time and patience in writing this book. I am truly grateful.

To Nicki Rensten (prison adviser): for her advice and support throughout the years on legalities; for listening and for being there.

To Eric Allison (*The Guardian*): for standing by me and supporting me with his articles.

Last but not least, I'm also thankful for all the friends who have stood by me throughout the years, giving me hope and helping me through the tough times. As you can imagine, it has been a very rocky and turbulent road but there have also been days of laughter, banter and companionship. I've met some very interesting people and made some good friends along the way:

Ashey, Azzopardi, Alan McCartney, Billy Gould (RIP), Benji, Branchy, Barry Morton, Charlie Bronson, Crofty, Cliff Moody, Carl Williams, Charlie Lawson, Charlie McGee (RIP), Chazz, Dave Annal, Damien Noonan (RIP), Derek Doyle, Dingus, Dave Pleasence, Delroy Shower, Darren Joans, Dave Dale, David Fields, Frank Burley (RIP), Eddie Slater, Frank Hughes, Glen Williams, George Hinds, Joe Murray, Jimmy Johnson, John Ives, Jimmy Gilmore, Jake, Jerry Scalease, John-John Murray, Jojo Collins, Kevin Gould, Kevin Lane, Kevin Carter, Kevin Brown, Kevin Whitehouse, Loz Brown, Mickey Steel, Mark Williams, Malcolm Sang, Nigel Robson, Parv Corkovic, Perry Warren, Paul Heaton, Ronnie Easterbrook (RIP), Steve Jonas, Sam Cole, Stephen, Nigel and Phil (RIP), Abbadon, Tony Bush, Tony Crab (RIP), Tony Buterill, Tony McCullack, Tony Steel, Tony, Mike, Lee Erdmann (RIP), Vince (RIP), Warren Taylor, Wayne Hurrin, Zaff, Mark Snell.

My apologies if I've missed anyone out, though I do have a very good excuse – it's called age! Keep your chin up, lads. If I can do it so can you...

CONTENTS

INTRODUCTION

For the past thirty-two years I've had something at the back of my mind, hidden away in one of those little memory boxes stored in your subconscious. When I looked back and thought of what happened to someone I'd known from my teenage years, it changed my mood and made me feel sad. He was a boy from the same area I lived in, north Manchester, who attended the same youth clubs as me in the late 1970s. We also shared the same taste in music and a circle of friends. He always seemed to be happy and polite; he was well dressed and very popular with the girls.

His name was Alan Lord, and he'd since become a convicted murderer. He was also involved in the worst prison riot in British history, at HMP Strangeways in 1990.

Alan was nineteen when he and his friends went out one night and committed a stupid act that would change their lives – especially his – forever. Worst of all, it ended in a man losing his life.

Alan was charged with murder in 1981, but throughout the years he kept trying to clear his name. There were too many inconsistencies surrounding the case. Had Alan Lord confessed under duress? Why was he interviewed without a solicitor present? Was he offered a phone call at any time? And what was the truth about his claim that he was beaten for several hours before he signed a statement he couldn't read properly, as his head was bent down to one side on the table whilst his hands were tied to the bottom of it? These allegations would be made in court when Alan finally had representation, but cut no ice with the jury. Instead, he got a life sentence that spanned thirty-two years in various prisons.

Alan had no intention of harming anyone, let alone causing a man's death. It was a mistake, a robbery gone badly wrong, a senseless spur-of-the-moment action that cost him thirty-two years of his life. Much of Alan's time was spent in the segregation unit, in solitary confinement, living in inhumane conditions without respect for human dignity. He also had to endure physical brutality and racial abuse on an almost daily basis.

I was young at the time but I never forgot what happened. I'd later read reports on the internet, after reading about his escapes and captures in the *Manchester Evening News* during 1990/93. I also read about the mistreatment and inhumane conditions he had to endure throughout his incarceration.

When I found out that Alan remained in prison in 2010, I couldn't believe he was still fighting the system after all those years. I wrote to Kingston Prison in June 2010 after a report that Alan was up for a parole board hearing, but received no reply.

After finding out from an old friend that Alan was still in prison in August 2012, I decided to find out where he was but had no luck. On 30 January 2013 I wrote to the prison service to find out if he'd been released or if he was still being held somewhere in the country. I wanted to contact Alan and write a book about his life experiences, to hear about the injustice, treatment and brutality he had endured during his time in prison, but most of all I wanted to find out about the crime he was alleged to have committed, as there were always rumours that he may have taken the rap for someone else. (Years later, a pathologist's report would suggest two bladed weapons were used against the victim – not just the knife that Alan was carrying.) I wanted to hear about his determination to change the way prisoners are treated and to stand up and fight for their human rights, no matter where they were incarcerated. But I couldn't find where Alan was and I didn't get a reply from the prison service. I wasn't going to give up but, at that moment in time, I had to put finding Alan to one side because of work commitments.

Then, in April 2013, I finally got in touch with Alan's niece, Yasmin, by chance on a social network. She told me he'd been released in December 2012, after being shipped around from prison to prison. I gave her my contact details for her to pass on and waited to see if Alan would get in touch with me. I didn't expect him to remember me from thirty-five years ago. I just hoped he wouldn't think I had anything to do with the prison service or that I was a reporter wanting an interview for a newspaper.

Of course, I didn't know if he'd want to drag up the past or for me to write a book about his life. I waited for a week but didn't hear anything, I just thought he probably didn't want to contact me and wasn't interested in anyone writing about what he'd been through. I felt a bit deflated, but contacted Yasmin one more time to ask if she'd sent my contact details to her uncle. To my surprise, she said he was going to get in touch with me.

Later that day I received a text message from Alan. He apologised for the delay and explained that he lived in Liverpool, and had just started working in a recycling plant. I texted him straight back and we made arrangements to meet up the following Sunday afternoon.

I was excited and had a good feeling about the whole project. We texted each other during the week, and I thought his messages sounded positive. But at the same time I felt a little apprehensive because I didn't know what to expect.

Sunday soon came around and I met Alan in The White Room, a wine and coffee shop in Whitefield, near to where I live. I felt anxious. I was worried about the state of mind Alan might still be in after all those years alone, confined to a small space, without contact with the outside world. I wondered how he was coping with all the changes, the noise of being around people, the new technology, or even public transport. I just didn't know what I was letting myself in for.

Before I could even contemplate writing this book, I had to ask Alan some very personal and intrusive questions. I needed him to trust and confide in me. I needed first of all to find out about the crime he was sentenced for, the murder charge. I had to ask him if there was any intent to kill someone – even though I knew deep down that would have made him psychotic, and I didn't believe he was a madman. I also had to find out if, after spending all those years in prison, he was of sound mind, or whether he was impaired by drugs or alcohol. If I was to write his autobiography, I needed him to be 100 per cent honest and tell me the truth in his own words.

As I walked into The White Room I recognised Alan straight away. He was sitting close to the front door; he looked huge, not the slim young boy at the youth club. It was obvious he'd been looking after himself and doing a lot of weight training.

Alan stood up to kiss my cheek and say hello. I didn't feel intimidated, although it was very strange to meet a convicted murderer. I was aware that some of my family and friends were concerned about me going to meet him alone; my sister even advised me to meet Alan in a very public place. But they need not have worried because I could see he was nervous and, in a funny kind of way, it made me feel relaxed.

I composed myself into professional mode and started talking about my work history and scriptwriting. The thought did run through my mind that I was facing one of the ringleaders of the worst prison riots in British history, but my anxiety vanished the minute I sat down to talk to him. Alan was polite, well-spoken and intelligent. We talked for four hours, and I knew there and then that I could write something to change people's perception of Alan Lord.

Alan confirmed he'd had no intent to commit the crime he was charged with, but he had confessed to murdering the man – although he maintained that the confession was made under duress, without any legal support, at Longsight Police Station. He stated that he'd never taken drugs in his life and had never been into drinking alcohol. He also confided in me the facts that you are about to read in this book – with which you will form your own opinion of Alan Lord, convicted murderer and riot leader.

From a very young age, Alan has always been in the wrong place at the wrong time, having had more than his fair share of bad luck and bad timing. But he has always stood up to the bitter end for what he believes in, to the point of sacrificing his own freedom.

Unlike the stereotypical thug portrayed in the national newspapers, Alan was a naive teenager who thought a life in petty crime would pay, after trying to find employment without any success. It all backfired one night when he and his friends went out to commit a robbery in a furniture shop.

Alan made the biggest mistake of his life when he put on the 'wrong coat' when leaving his friend's house in a rush. The dark blue coat (similar to his black one) contained a lock knife hidden in the pocket to protect himself from a rival gang in Salford, who had stopped him on Waterloo Road, Cheetham Hill, a few nights earlier. But on the night in question it was early evening, around 5.30, when he set off, so he should have known he was safe at that time.

In the modern legal environment, Alan Lord would have been charged with manslaughter, not murder. There was no intent to commit murder as the robbery was a purely opportunistic crime.

Deep down, Alan is not even sure if it was him or one of his so-called friends who caused the man's death, but he has to live with recurring images of that fateful night for the rest of his life. He also had to live with inhumane treatment for over thirty-two years, locked away for twenty-three out of twenty-four hours a day, taking as little as possible from the regime so that they couldn't take anything back as a punishment. All Alan had in his cell was a sheet on the floor, not even a bed, and his toiletries neatly packed away for any sudden move.

Alan would later become a figurehead, and perhaps scapegoat, for the HMP Strangeways riot in Manchester, because he took part in a collective decision to protest against the regime and the inhumane conditions. It was time for change; time for someone to stand up and say enough is enough. But he received no recognition for keeping the peace whilst on the roof, encouraging young offenders to hand themselves in before they got swept off by water cannons as prison officers looked on from the windows, laughing and taunting the prisoners. Alan wrote messages on boards so that the press and public would know the truth about how prisoners were treated behind closed doors, and was given a further ten years for his part in the protest.

Anita Armstrong

32 YEARS LOCKED AWAY IN PRISON

In order of incarceration:

Her Majesty's Prison Strangeways, Manchester – 1981

HMP Wakefield, Yorkshire – 1981

HMP Durham – 1982

HMP Leicester – 1982 (Night stops)

HMP Gartree, Leicester – 1982

HMP Bullingdon, Bicester – 1982 (Night stops)

HMP Birmingham – 1982

HMP Wandsworth, London – 1982 (Night stops)

HMP Strangeways, Manchester – 1982

HMP Durham – 1982–3

HMP Frankland, Durham – late 1983–9

HMP Garth, Preston – 1989

LIFE IN STRANGEWAYS

HMP Strangeways, Manchester – 1989–90

Astley Bridge Police Station, Bolton,
 Greater Manchester – 1990

HMP Wakefield, Yorkshire – 1990

HMP Frankland – 1990–1

HMP Hull Prison – 1991

HMP Parkhurst, Isle of Wight – late 1991

HMP Full Sutton, Yorkshire – 1991–2

HMP Parkhurst, Isle of Wight – 1992–3

HMP Whitemoor, Cambridge – 1993

HMP Hull – 1993–4

HMP Durham – 1994–6

HMP Whitemoor, Cambridge – 1996

HMP Doncaster – 1996–7

HMP Long Lartin, Evesham – 1997

HMP Woodhill, Kent – 1997

HMP Doncaster – late 1997

HMP Full Sutton, Yorkshire – late 1997

HMP Bristol – late 1998

HMP Doncaster – late 1998–9

HMP Frankland – 1999–2004

HMP Dovegate, Uttoxeter – 2004–6

HMP Kingston, Portsmouth – 2006–10

HMP Winchester – late 2010

HMP Rye Hill, Rugby – 2011

HMP Buckley Hall, Rochdale, Greater Manchester – 2011

HMP Risley, Warrington, Greater Manchester – 2011–12

HMP Sudbury, Derbyshire – 2012–13

CHAPTER ONE

FREEDOM
OF SPEECH

My name is Alan Lord and, for the first time in thirty-two years, I feel I have a voice.

Freedom of speech is a wonderful thing, but I will never be free from the stigma of being labelled a convicted murderer. I am not a murderer and should never have been convicted of the offence. I did not intend to take the life of David Gilbert and to this day I do not know if it was actually me who ended Mr Gilbert's life in 1981.

But I am truly and deeply sorry for the hurt I caused to Mr Gilbert and his family. I am ashamed of the actions I took that fateful night because, I admit, I *did* try to take his briefcase from him, I *did* have a knife in my hand to try to frighten him and I *did* cause injuries to Mr Gilbert while we were fighting. If I could turn back time I would, but that is not possible. I was a hot-headed, mixed-up nineteen-year-old who got involved with the wrong crowd and thought a life of crime would pay. How stupid and naive I was!

I am not saying I did not deserve to be punished; I hold my hands up and admit that my actions could have caused Mr Gilbert's death – or that is what I was led to believe after being interrogated for several hours and having it drummed into me. I admitted to the crime under extreme pressure. Looking back now over the surrounding circumstances, the fatal blows may even have been struck by one of my so-called pals, but I took the rap.

It was never my intention to end his life though, and I should have been handed a manslaughter sentence – not murder, even though manslaughter sounds more gruelling. Yes, I went to take his briefcase, but I was defending myself when he hit out at me and a fight broke out. I am not saying Mr Gilbert was in the wrong and I am not making excuses; it was *me* who was in the wrong, it was *me* who had the knife in my hand and it was *me* who was going to steal from him. But I didn't expect him to hit out at me and I never expected myself to retaliate in the way that I did, possibly causing his death.

I am not writing this book for profit, publicity or the respect of other prison inmates – past or present – who may think I'm some kind of hero for my involvement in the HMP Strangeways riots. Back then, I was only trying to make the public aware of what was going on behind closed doors, of the inhumane treatment and brutalising of prisoners, and the lack of respect shown towards their families.

By writing this book I hope I can change the path of young people who think a life of crime pays, when all that will happen is that they serve a long time behind bars, leaving their loved ones and families devastated. If I can change just one person's perception of a life lived in dishonesty and prison cells, then this book will not have been written in vain.

Losing your freedom and dignity, and seeing your family once a month, if you're lucky, is not worth any amount of material gain. I've lost friends who took the wrong turning that led them to alcohol and drug abuse. I've been confined with men who are going to die in prison, who have no hope of ever being released, and I've seen the blank expressions on their faces. We all know that life can sometimes be hard, but the world is full of opportunities and they are there for the taking.

As I sit at home, looking out of the window at the trees blowing in the wind, the keys to the front door still clenched in my hand, for the first time in thirty-two years I feel a sense of peace in complete silence. There is no banging of doors, no lock-up, no shouting and screaming, no listening to screws' derogatory comments, no inmates playing loud music to vibrate through the ceiling and down my cell walls. It's a strange feeling because it's an outer peace that surrounds me. I will never have inner peace because of the anxiety and guilt that rushes through me whenever I think of the past; sometimes the remorse just eats away at my insides, leaving me feeling withdrawn. I try to lift my spirits by going for long walks and with my daily routine of weights and circuit training.

I sometimes think about what should have – could have, would have – been, but I just push those thoughts away and think of the here and now. That is how I got through all those years of incarceration. Otherwise it can turn a man to madness and, believe me, I've witnessed many men losing it inside and heading straight to the mental ward. That was one place I never wanted to go – even though there were plenty of screws who would have loved to see me in there, or in a wooden box. I just stayed focused on the straight and narrow, working out, building my physique and avoiding drugs or homemade prison juice (hooch).

I'm out of prison but I'll never be free from the restrictions and limitations I have to adhere to for the rest of my life. I have a life licence until the day I die. I am forever looking over my shoulder, trying to avoid even the slightest confrontation on a daily basis. I have no wife, no children and I'm too old to start a family. I have nowhere I can call home; I have no real identity, I've never been out of the country and will never be able to hold a British passport. This is my sacrifice; I took the wrong path and paid the price.

I will never know what it is like to feel real freedom, even though I've served my time. I have to be thankful that I can now at last feel the fresh air, and see the sunshine beaming down; even the wind and rain on my face feels exhilarating whenever I go walking in the park or to the local shops, like a little piece of heaven no one can take away.

CHAPTER TWO

THE EARLY YEARS

As I looked out of the window I could see an old couple walking past. I thought of my parents, and then of my sister and myself as young children. I looked back on my childhood and tried to remember when things started going wrong for me. But I just couldn't think of anything I did as a young boy to make my life turn out so bad.

As I thought about my younger years and looked back as far as I possibly could, I had a vision of myself sitting in my high chair as a toddler. My sister Eunice was rocking back and forth on her rocking horse across the room from me; I remember her looking over with her brown eyes and big smile, shouting at me as she went faster and faster, laughing out loud. I was a little bit frightened that she might go flying off her rocking horse as she was going very fast, but at the same time she was making me laugh.

Then we heard a loud bang in the hallway and looked towards the door. Eunice's expression had changed from laughter to fear. We could hear our mother scream, then the door flew open and she came running into the room, blood dripping from her nose, covering her hands and face. Our father soon followed her in, hitting her and kicking her to the ground in front of us. My sister was screaming and crying as our father carried on beating our mother. I sat there transfixed, wishing and hoping it would soon stop and he'd just go upstairs or go out.

That kind of violence and abuse was a regular occurrence in our house. Our mother took some beatings but so did we – only my sister and I were too young to run away, unlike our mother who often left us at home with our father and his wooden stick. He was very strict and had some old-fashioned values.

My sister and I did not have a good start in life. Our parents were both in their forties when we were born and did not seem to take much interest in us. We didn't know what it was like to have a real family home, but then we were taken to four children's homes and seven foster homes before I was ten years old. I always thought there was someone worse off than myself and felt sorry for the children in the homes who had no mother and father, and the children who had been abused by their parents or some other monster. I would paint a picture in my mind of my sister and I having a normal, happy childhood – but then I felt ashamed and embarrassed that we had no love or affection, and were placed in care homes because our parents didn't want us. Or at least it felt that way.

I remember being placed with a family of funeral directors, Mr and Mrs Egan, who lived in Moston, Manchester. Mrs Egan was a lovely lady who looked after my sister and I for quite some time. They had two sons and two daughters but I was too young to remember their names; I just felt happy to be part of a family who cared for us. Sadly, it was only temporary because we ended up going back home, but I'll always have good memories of my time with them.

In fact I sometimes block out the terrible periods I had at home and think about the rare good times with my father. My mother was too cold to care, but I remember my father taking me to the park and kicking a ball around with me; it was nice to have him take some interest. I also remember a time when he was cleaning the windows at home and letting me climb on the bottom step of his ladder while he cleaned at the top. It was remembering things like that let me push the bad times to the back of my mind. I also remembered a very rare occasion when my mother and father bought a bike for my tenth birthday. I could not believe it, I was so excited. I remember my mother walking up the street with my bike; I ran over to her, jumped straight on it and sped off.

My sister and I were played off against each other most of the time by our parents, and when it suited them we were supposed to slot into their imaginary happy family. It was when they were full of booze that the arguments would start, and we got all the blame just for being around.

I also remember being taken to the Strawberry Fields Salvation Army children's home in Liverpool with my sister, where we stayed for quite a long time. It had been made famous by John Lennon when he wrote the song 'Strawberry Fields Forever'. I met a boy at the home who was the same age as me and we became very good friends. I'll never forget when he went missing for a few days. I was wondering where he was and asking the other children, but they didn't know either. I went all over the home looking for him.

Then, in a room on the top floor where the door was always closed, I opened it and there he was – sitting in the dark with socks wrapped round his hands, tied with tape, crying.

I was so frightened for him that I ran out of the house to find a policeman. One of the other children told a carer and she came running to bring me back. I thought that was it – I was going to be tied up too. But she took me back and sat me down in the office, asking why I was running away. I told her about my friend. She smiled and told me not to worry: he had a bad spell of dry eczema and had to be bathed in lotion. The socks were to stop him scratching his sores and the darkness was to protect him from the irritation of the lights. I was so relieved because I'd thought it was some kind of punishment. The carer let me go and sit with him for a while as his temperature had come down and his sores had stopped bleeding.

In fact I liked the children's home in Liverpool. It was the first time in my childhood that I felt settled. The carers who looked after me were very compassionate, and I was so happy that I had a good friend to share my days with. I remember walking to school with some of the children down a road lined with trees. I started doing well in school. Then, one day, my mother and father turned up for me. I didn't want to go home but my parents played happy families. The head of the home and social services fell for their lies, so I had to go with them. I guess they had got back together after a recent split, but I just couldn't understand why they took me home and left my sister there.

I was only home for a few days before the arguments started again. I'd already had enough of the cold atmosphere and loneliness, and needed to find a way to get back to the Salvation Army home. I couldn't stand the silent treatment I got from my mother or my father's rules and regulations. So I ran away and found my way back to Liverpool. I don't know how I got there but I did.

Once back in the town I knew I looked at the road signs and started to recognise the streets. I was hungry and tired when I finally got there, as I'd had to take shelter a few times along the way: in doorways, under a bridge, I even remember waking up in a coal bunker at the side of someone's house.

I think it took me about five days to find the home. When I finally got through the famous gates of Strawberry Fields, I ran into the grounds and climbed up a tree. I looked through the windows to see if I could see my friend, but the groundsman saw me and told me to get down, taking me inside to the office. The carers were very surprised to see me back and couldn't believe I'd actually found my way back to the home on my own. One of them said I was like a stray cat that returned because he'd been looked after and fed well.

But I was upset when they made a phone call to my father and told him where I was. He soon came for me and took me back down the M60 motorway, back to Manchester. I was punished for days on end for embarrassing him. I couldn't understand why my sister was left at Strawberry Fields and I had to go home, but then she always said they didn't like her and didn't want her. She had a very tough time growing up in various children's homes. I remember my father beating her badly with a stick once in front of people in the street where we lived. Nothing was ever done.

I couldn't settle at home and started being rebellious: running away, staying at friends' houses and telling lies to their parents so that I could stay over. But I was soon found out and back in trouble again, punished with the belt or stick, and grounded. I remember trying not to upset my parents for a while and following their rules, obeying my father's orders. I started gaining trust, even being allowed to have my own front-door key.

Then, one day in the school holidays, I went home for something to eat and took my friends with me. We stayed in the backyard most of the day, but there was a boy who came with one of my friends who I didn't really know that well. I tried to keep my eye on him but he left early. Later that day, we all went out to the park before my parents returned home, as they wouldn't allow my friends into the house.

The next morning my father shouted my name out loud. I knew by the tone of his voice that I was in some kind of trouble. When I got downstairs he was stood there with his stick in his hand. He started screaming at me. 'Get down here!' he shouted, and started chasing me around the room hitting me with the stick and shouting at the top of his voice. 'Where is the clock?'

I told him I didn't know what he was talking about, but he just kept hitting me. He told me to find who'd taken the clock and bring it back. I couldn't get it back and was never trusted again. I had my door key taken off me and was locked out of the house from early in the morning until my parents came home at six in the evening. I had to go all day sometimes without anything to eat, and find somewhere to take cover from the rain if my friends were not at home.

Being at home was what I hated, and my sister was never there. I just got blanked whenever I asked where she was. It was a horrible atmosphere. My parents hardly said two words to each other and I just kept running away. I remember staying in the park. I went to find some wood to make a fire, as I didn't want to spend another cold night in the doorway of the bowling green around the corner. I was walking back when I saw the figure of a man coming towards me.

I was so frightened that I started running, but he was getting closer and closer. I thought he was going to kill me but, when I looked again, I could see it was a police officer chasing me. He soon caught up and grabbed hold of my coat.

'Come 'ere, you little black bastard!' he shouted, and started dragging me across the bowling green. 'What do you think you are doing 'ere, you little shit?'

'Hiding,' I said.

He asked me where I lived and took me home. In one way I was glad I was found, because I was beginning to get really hungry. I didn't know what was worse, the hunger pains or the pain of my father's stick when I got home.

The police officer told my parents he found me trying to light a fire in the park; he also told my mother he'd have to inform social services because my parents hadn't told the police I was missing and I'd been away from home for three nights. I soon became a ward of court for my own protection and safety. My parents told the police and the courts that I was a disruptive child and they could not control me, and my running away was nothing to do with them. But I wasn't out of control or disruptive; I was a thirteen-year-old who needed a bit of attention and a little TLC, just like any other child of that age needs.

CHAPTER THREE

THE REBELLIOUS YEARS

At age thirteen I was taken back into care and placed in Broom House, a children's home, until they found a placement for me. I was only there for a few weeks before I was sent to Rose Hill, a boys' home not only for disruptive, out-of-control children, but also for those who'd gone through the juvenile courts for petty crimes. I was thrown in the deep end and had to grow up fast. There were older boys in there and the physical abuse came not only from the bullies at Rose Hill, but was also dished out by some of the carers – the very people who were supposed to protect the boys.

I remember one day while I was waiting in the dinner line, one of the bullies who everyone was scared of started poking the younger boys in the face. They had made it clear that they were in charge and had their own way of intimidating us. They used to wrap nylon string around their hands and snap it fast in front of the boys' faces to frighten them. When the bully came up to me I punched him hard and knocked him to the floor, then ran out of the dining room as fast as I could. I ran into the woods surrounding Rose Hill, where four teachers – including two brothers who I hated – soon followed me.

So I ran as fast as I could but they caught up with me and knocked me to the floor, hitting me with sticks. One of them was kicking me all over while the other was holding me down. They hit me on the backs of my legs, calling me a black bastard. I was screaming and shouting at them to leave me alone but they just carried on.

Then they dragged me back to the home and pushed me into the dorm, shutting the door. I got straight into bed, still in clothes caked with mud. I wrapped myself in the blankets and did not wake up until the next day. I was in a lot of pain and badly bruised, my eyes all swollen and red, but none of the carers blinked an eyelid when I went down for breakfast.

I was in Rose Hill for around three months; it was a terrible time for me. I remember when Mrs Egan came to visit me; she was upset and told me she was sorry she didn't keep me with her as a foster mother. But she said it was out of her hands and I'd had to go back home to my parents, yet again.

So I stayed in Rose Hill until I was moved to Mobberely Boys' Home; they had their own way of welcoming new recruits at Mobberely, it was a whole new ball game. I had to become tougher and stand up for myself. I became more boisterous and rebellious, because yet again I found myself facing physical and racial abuse. But this time it was different. I started to fight back and became more disruptive; I had to show the lads I was not going to put up with it any longer.

It was at Mobberely Boys' Home that I met a boy called Kane Clarke, something which I would regret for the rest of my life. Kane became a friend because we had similar backgrounds. We'd both suffered the same abuse at the hands of the so-called care system. Mobberely was a very cold and regimented place; there was a lot of bullying going on and not just from the older lads, the staff did their fair share of handing out the punishment. It was just like at Rose Hill but on a much larger scale. I had to walk tall and put on a front as far as the bullies were concerned. But then I tried to avoid the staff by staying out of their way and blending into the background.

Sometimes I just wanted to be on my own and would go out into the fields to feel the fresh air on my face. It was good to see the open fields and the animals on the nearby farm; even though I was a city boy I loved to be close to nature. I'd climb under the fence and go into the farmer's field without anyone knowing. I just wanted some peace away from all that was going on inside Mobberely.

I remember one day walking through the farm. As the cows in the field came towards me, I started walking fast to get away from them. The faster I was walking the faster the cows trotted. I started running and, when I turned round, the cows were chasing me, so I jumped over some hedges that separated the farm and the fields near the edge of Mobberely and landed in a deep stream. I was wet through and had to walk all the way back, soaking wet with my boots full of mud. When I finally got back to Mobberely, I tried to sneak in but I got caught. Not only did the boys take the piss out of me for looking like a drowned rat, but I got punished for the state I was in and the mess I'd made walking through the dorms. As soon as I got showered and changed, I was sent for and got a good beating with the cane. This time it was not just on my hands and legs that I received the lashes, but my backside. It was a bit sore to sit on for a few days.

After that I decided I wanted to leave Mobberely. I ran away on my own early one morning. I didn't tell anyone I was going just in case they wanted to come with me, which would have turned it into a mission. I packed a few things in a small bag and put on my donkey jacket, which made me look a little bit older than my fifteen years. I started walking down a country lane but didn't get very far before I was stopped by a police car. I guess I must have stood out like a sore thumb. I thought if I put on a deep voice and pretended I was on my way to work it'd be fine, but it didn't work. I knew I was in trouble and was going to be taken back, so I jumped over the fields and ran as fast as I could. When I looked back the police car was nowhere to be seen; it felt good that I'd got away.

I sat down for a while in the overgrown grass until I thought it was safe to carry on. Then I made my way to my sister's house, as by now she was living in Victoria Square in the city centre of Manchester. I walked all the way, mostly through fields, then found myself on Princess Parkway and walked straight down into town. Looking back, I was a little bit stupid because my sister's house was the first place they would look for me. It wasn't long before they took me back to Mobberely.

I was becoming more disruptive and had got involved with some boys who were popular at Mobberely, including Kane. It felt good to have a group of friends to banter with; we got up to all sorts of pranks, mostly on each other, and I felt like I could fit in with like-minded boys who seemed carefree.

Another time that I planned to run away, I got some of the boys to come with me. We'd all had enough of Mobberely and one of the boys wanted to get back to Wythenshawe, Greater Manchester, to see a family member who was having some problems. So off we went.

We started walking towards Manchester Airport. It was very dark and we needed to get as far away from Mobberely as possible. One lad noticed a Land Rover parked on a farmer's driveway and one of the others, who was good at hot-wiring cars, said he could get it started if we got in and took the handbrake off, rolling the car off the driveway. So we got in – two in the front, two in the back – without any disturbance, waited until we were down the road to start it up and one of the boys drove us all to Wythenshawe. On the way out of Mobberely, we pulled over on a dirt track to throw a riding saddle out; we found out weeks later that it was worth a lot of money. I was gutted!

But it was good to get away from Mobberely, and we had such a good laugh. How we didn't get caught I'll never know.

We got to Wythenshawe and parked the car in a side street; we left the keys still in the engine and went our separate ways. I headed back to my sister's again; I guess it was the only place I could go to and where I could get my head down and some food to eat.

Looking back, it seems I was always running away from somewhere or someone. Maybe it was a cry for help, or the feeling of attention I got from knowing there was someone out there who could be bothered to look for me. Or maybe it was the adrenalin boost I got from trying to avoid getting caught.

I had to put up with the racial abuse I endured from some of the staff at Mobberely, who were there supposedly to support, protect and care for me. I've since taken legal action against the children's homes which resulted in an out-of-court settlement. But maybe it was the colour of my skin and my rebelliousness that saved me from the sexual abuse rumoured to be going in the dorms late at night.

It was quite disturbing to think of something like that and I often wondered how I'd react if I got a night call. It made me feel sick and anxious whenever I heard the dorm door open in the middle of the night; I'd always hide under my blanket and get ready to punch someone hard in the face if they dared come near me. We continuously hear of such vile practices committed by people who should be caring for children, not abusing them, and despite the authorities' rhetoric it is still going on today – as it has been throughout the centuries.

I was sixteen when I left Mobberely to live with my sister in Manchester city centre. I also stayed at Kane Clarke's house in Cheetham Hill from time to time. It was good to be able to do whatever I wanted. I got a job working at a garage in Ardwick Green, near to my parents' house; I wanted to be a mechanic and went to Openshaw College, close to the centre of Manchester. I started earning money and bought my first car. I also enjoyed going out with Kane to Abraham Moss youth club and other clubs local to where he lived. I started seeing girls and we went out to various nightclubs in Manchester city centre, even though we were well underage; it was the late 1970s and going clubbing was the 'in' thing. I was never into alcohol or drugs, and have never smoked; I was just there for the music and, obviously, the girls.

Whilst hanging around on the Waterloo estate, I met Paul Flannery and Mike Sharples and all four of us started hanging around together. We became good friends and spent a lot of time getting up to the kinds of things teenagers did in those days. The only one of them I'm still in contact with today is Paul. I always knew he'd do well for himself, because he was highly motivated and set his goals high. Paul was always a good businessman and I have much respect for him.

For the first time in my life I felt I had some direction. I felt happy and contented. I had my college course and my job; I was getting on my feet; I started seeing a girl from Withington and staying over at her house from time to time. I was still staying at Kane's house and at my sister's, but I wanted to find a place of my own now that I was working and earning money. But I never got the chance because my life turned upside down again.

One day I went to my parents' house to get some clothes and my records. My father had been out drinking and was in a foul mood; he didn't even acknowledge me when I walked into the room. I tried to start a conversation with him and tell him I was looking to get my own place, thinking he'd be proud of me for getting on with my life, but he went mad, shouting at me at the top of his voice: 'Who do you think you are, treating this house like a hotel?'

I think he thought I was going to come back home. He shouted at me again and we started arguing. I was answering him back, something I'd never have dared to do in the past.

And my father went crazy. He ran into the kitchen, got a claw hammer out of the drawer and ran after me. I fled upstairs to get out of his way and he chased me. I was so frightened; I really thought he was going to hit me over the head. I got halfway up the stairs and took hold of a small statue on the landing shelf, throwing it down at my father to stop him coming after me with the hammer. It caught him and cut his forehead.

My mother was screaming at my father to stop it, but he started coming after me again. Then there was a knocking at the front door and he went down to answer it, and I could hear the neighbour asking if everything was okay. I grabbed some clothes out of my room and ran out fast.

I went to my girlfriend's house in Withington; I had to walk all the way because I'd dropped my money while trying to get out of the house. By the time I got to Withington she told me the police had been there, looking for me, so I took off straight away to Kane's house. I told him what had happened and he told me to stay there with him until it calmed down. I felt bad that I'd caught my father on the head with the object I threw but I just didn't know why he was so aggressive with me.

That night Kane and I went out to the Duke pub in Cheetham Hill, on the Waterloo Road estate. We were sat in the pub, talking to some of the lads from the estate and Kane was drinking, when the landlord came over and asked me to leave if I wasn't going to buy a drink. He was poking his finger at me and getting verbal, so I told him where to go. He tried to grab hold of me to throw me out. I warned him to get off but he wouldn't let go, so I punched him in the face and knocked him to the floor.

I left the pub, smashing a window on the way out. I didn't realise I had a bad cut to my hand until I got outside; it was quite deep so Kane and I went to North Manchester General Hospital.

While we were in the waiting area I was approached by the landlord's wife. She was shouting at me and telling me her husband was having treatment in a side ward, screaming that it was all my fault. The next minute, two police officers came over to find out what all the commotion was about; she started telling the police that I'd assaulted her husband; I couldn't get a word in to explain that he'd started the argument and provoked the fight. I wasn't given a chance to explain, and when I gave my name they already had a warrant out for my arrest for assaulting my father.

So I was also arrested for assaulting the landlord. I was taken to Collyhurst Police Station without receiving any treatment, even though my hand was badly cut; I just had to wrap my top around it to stop the bleeding. When I got to the station I was charged with grievous bodily harm on my father and assault on the pub landlord. My dad later told me it was the next-door neighbour who had called the police, but it was too late. He'd made a statement and the police pressed charges for both offences, for which I'd be sentenced to six months in prison.

CHAPTER FOUR

FIRST TASTE
OF PRISON LIFE

I was placed in HMP Strangeways, Manchester, for four weeks, and then spent ten more in Preston Prison. I didn't have any visitors. I'd lost my job, my college course and my girlfriend. I felt like I'd been put in prison just for defending myself: first against my abusive father and then against the pub landlord who'd given me his bad attitude, poking and embarrassing me in front of my friends.

Then I was put into the segregation unit after a few weeks for fighting with a Scottish inmate. He threw hot tea in my face when I asked him to clear his slop bucket out because it was overflowing. We were forced to share a small cell but I was very clean and tidy. I didn't want to share my personal space with a smelly tramp.

I was released from Preston just before my nineteenth

birthday. I went to stay at my sister's house and, after a short time, Kane came round to see me. I was a bit pissed off with him at first, as he couldn't be bothered to come and visit me while I was in Preston, or even send me a postcard. But I let bygones be bygones, even though I'd have been there for him – at that time anyway, not anymore. I guess you just have to live and learn and find out who your real friends are.

Next I tried to get a job but it was hard with a prison record. I started going out with Kane and some of the other lads off the Waterloo Road estate to do petty crime. We never hurt anyone and we never burgled people's homes. I knew it was wrong but I had to make money somehow. I didn't go out robbing to feed a habit; I did it to be able to buy food and clothes, the basics. I couldn't sign on because I had no fixed address and I had no support from my family. What else could I do?

Then one day I went out with Kane and some of his cronies and did something stupid, which would completely change my life forever. I was staying at his house in the middle of winter, 1981; it was thick with snow outside and all I wanted to do was stay in and keep warm, as I had a cold.

Kane had gone out before I got up that morning, so I just stayed in all day watching the television. He came back later that day, around 5.30, and said he was going back out with the Ikegulu brothers – Chuck, Eric, and Mac – to rob a furniture shop on Cheetham Hill Road. He asked me to go with him. I was unsure what to do; my instincts were telling me not to go, and I didn't want to go out in the thick snow and cold. I told Kane I was going to leave it and stay in and watch *The Dukes of Hazzard* on television. I didn't feel too good, but in the end he coaxed me into going with him. I guess loyalty got the better of me.

I got my coat from the hallway, forgetting that I'd put a lock knife in the pocket. I'd bought it a few days earlier from a shop at the side of Piccadilly train station in Manchester. I'd previously been stopped at the bottom of Waterloo Road, the division between Salford and Cheetham Hill, by a gang in a black car who chased me through the estate. It had happened a couple of times when I was on my own, but the last time, when I was with Kane, we went to confront them but they had weapons. Kane was a faster runner than me and I soon fell behind. One of the boys nearly caught up with me and I could clearly see he had a flick knife in his hand. I managed to get away but decided that I'd never leave myself in a situation again where I couldn't defend myself.

Of course I had no intention of ever using the knife. I just wanted to show them I could stand up for myself, because I felt like a coward running away. Looking back now, it brought me more trouble than I could ever have imagined. I do believe now that if you carry a weapon – a knife, gun, whatever – you are at risk of serious injury, of losing your life or the life of someone else.

We left Kane's house to meet the Ikegulu brothers not far from where he lived. We walked up Cheetham Hill Road to the furniture shop but when we got there it had already closed. We hadn't made any plans, I just knew one of the brothers was going into the shop to take the money from the till while the rest of us watched out, but we had to leave it.

So we started walking up Cheetham Hill Road to get something to eat. I put my hand in my pockets for some change, and that's when I realised I'd put my dark blue coat on instead of the black one. I had no money in my pockets, only the knife.

As we walked up towards the kebab shop at the top end of the road, we noticed two men locking up a jewellery shop on the opposite side. One of them had a briefcase in his hand and started walking towards Wilton Polygon. The other man went in the opposite direction. One of the Ikegulu brothers said, 'I bet he's got jewellery or watches in his case.' So the brothers held back while Kane and I followed him.

I walked slowly in front of Kane and caught up with the man. I couldn't believe he couldn't see or hear me but it was thick with snow. I took out the knife just to frighten him into handing me the case. I walked faster to catch up with him and tapped him on the shoulder. But before I could finish saying, 'Give me your briefcase,' he turned round fast and swung the case in my face.

In fact I can't remember if it was the briefcase or his fist that hit me first, but I reacted with a punch and we started fighting. I was sliding all over the place in the snow, then he slipped and dragged me down with him. I jumped up fast to get away because by this time I was on my own. The lads had all run off, leaving me behind.

It all happened so fast, the adrenalin was working over-time, it felt so surreal. I just wanted to get away before someone saw me and called the police.

Next I managed to get up and run down the road, I looked

back to see if the man was chasing me, but he was brushing the snow off himself. It was when I started running across Bury New Road that I realised I still had the knife in my hand. I panicked when I remembered hitting him with my hand, because when I looked closely at the knife there was a small spot of blood on the end. But then I checked my clothes and boots, and I had no blood on me whatsoever, not even a speck, so I thought he'd be okay.

I didn't see anyone take the briefcase, but one of the lads must have come back because there was no sign of it when I stood up. I ran as fast as I could down Waterloo Road to my sister's house.

Not long after I got there, Kane and the Ikegulu brothers came banging on the door. They were shouting at me because they heard on the news that a man had been murdered near Wilton Polygon, where the robbery had taken place.

I was frozen with fear and felt sick inside. I'd no idea I'd even injured the man, let alone killed him. I knew he was alive when I left the scene because I saw him stand up before I ran away. But Kane was saying he was not going down for murder and the Ikegulu brothers were getting very vocal, telling me to hand myself in and trying to shift the blame onto me when it was them who instigated the robbery in the first place.

And I felt betrayed by their reaction, isolated and singled out. I still don't know what really happened to this day. It all happened so fast, but it was me who had the knife in my hand and it was me who went to take the briefcase off him – even though it was one of my supposed friends who took it

27

from him when he went down in the snow – so I had to stand up and face whatever was coming to me.

While I was arguing with the lads in my sister's kitchen, she came in and asked us all to leave. She had a new baby in the house and was worried about the police coming through her front door, as she'd heard what had happened. So we went our separate ways.

I went with Kane to his house. He told me he'd got the briefcase and had hidden it somewhere. I wasn't interested in the case at that time; I just wanted to find out how the man could have died. I was devastated and confused.

Later on, we went to the Duke pub on the estate to find out if anyone had heard anything. I was told the police were looking for me. I didn't know what to do. I was wondering who had grassed me up. I was in a panic, full of a cold, and felt so ill and weak. I knew I was in a lot of trouble and didn't know how I could get out of the situation.

I left Kane and ran over to the house of a friend of mine, Julie, who lived near the Gospel Church on the estate. In her house I looked through the window and saw police officers coming out of a house across the way. I stayed in Julie's for a while until I thought the police had gone.

In the end I eventually left and went across the road to ask the neighbours what the police were saying. As I walked round the corner I could see three unmarked police cars with plainclothes officers stood around. I also noticed Kane's dog near a police officer.

I carried on walking across the road because I thought if I doubled back I'd look suspicious. I kept my head down, hoping Kane's dog wouldn't recognise me, but when I looked over at him he was wagging his tail and started coming towards me. I started whistling a UB40 song because I didn't want the police to notice I was nervous.

Next I walked up the maisonette stairs, acting cool like I lived there and was going home. I had to walk past Julie's friends' house, where I was intending to go, because the police officers were stood underneath. I walked along the landing, right to the end, and noticed two police cars driving off and turning left, before another one followed behind. It looked like all three police cars had gone, but then the last one slowed down and did a U-turn. I stood watching it speed up towards the flats. I knew one of the officers inside the car had noticed me, as he pointed to where I was and looked straight at me. I ran down the stairs and hid in the refuse area, because there was nowhere else to run to. I didn't want to get caught before I found out what had happened to the man who died in the robbery. I just couldn't believe I was responsible. I felt terrified and very hollow inside. I knew once I was caught that would be it. I was going to be locked away for a very long time.

I could hear police officers coming towards me while I was hiding in the refuse shed, getting closer and closer. Then the door opened and I was dragged out by the scruff of my neck.

'Come out, you murdering little black bastard!'

I was marched over to the police car. One of the officers grabbed hold of my top and tried to push me in. I stiffened and stood up straight.

Then I noticed around five lads coming over. One

recognised me and asked me what was going on, but the police officer who had hold of me told them to go away. One lad told me the officer was pulling a stick from behind his back. I just lost it and tried to get him off me.

We struggled. I got loose and pushed him to the side to get away. He slipped and fell to the floor, hit his head on the pavement and was knocked out.

I ran off towards the adventure playground, then back to Julie's house where I knew it would be safe for a while. But before I got near I noticed heads popping up and down behind the walls. I was caught out.

So I ran as fast as I could towards the Apollo pub on the estate and jumped over a wall into someone's back garden. I was soon followed by a plainclothes officer; as he climbed over I dragged him down to the floor, punched him in the face and jumped back over the other side of the wall – right into the middle of about ten police officers.

There was no getting away this time. I was grabbed, and pinned to the floor. I was trodden on and had racial abuse shouted down my ears.

I was thrown in the back of a police van with my hands handcuffed behind my back, followed by around eight police officers who attacked me. They were all screaming abuse at me and taking it in turns to stamp on me, laughing all the way to Longsight Police Station.

When we eventually got to the station I was dragged out of the van, still handcuffed. They lifted me up in the air and carried me through the station, throwing me on the floor in the corridor. The person who was leading the investigation walked up and said to one of the police officers, 'Kick that black bastard in the balls!'

I was frightened and didn't know what they were going to do to me. I was dragged into an interview room struggling, but it was no good. The more I struggled, the more digs I got. It was hopeless, there were just too many of them. I couldn't move and the handcuffs were cutting into my wrists. I was handcuffed to a footstool with my head pressed down on the table in a very awkward position. My neck was twisted to one side and I was repeatedly struck while being interviewed by the CS.

No solicitor was present to help me and I was never asked if I wanted one. The interview went on for quite some time, during which the CS told me the Ikegulu brothers had made a statement that I was the one who murdered David Gilbert and they had nothing to do with it. That was the first time I heard the man's name.

While I had my head pressed down onto the table, a forensics officer came into the room and yanked some of the hair out of my head. He then stuck a needle in my arm and took a blood sample. I was not told what was happening to me; he just walked in and out without any explanation.

I continued to be questioned for several hours without a break. I had a police officer shouting, 'You murdered him!' repeatedly down my ear. They were saying I'd stabbed Mr Gilbert in the back, but I just couldn't think straight. In the end I shouted out loud, 'Okay, I did it, I stabbed him!'

One of the officers asked, 'Where?' I replied, 'I stabbed him in the back.' I said it because that is what they were repeating to me time and time again, I said it just to get out of there, but the truth is that I really didn't know if I'd stabbed Mr Gilbert. It was all a blur.

All they wanted me to do was to confess. I just wanted it to stop. I was tired and drained and at that time I really didn't know if I'd inflicted any fatal stab wounds. All I wanted to do was close my eyes and not wake up.

At that point I was told I had to make a statement. The CS went out of the room with a big smirk on his face. He'd got what he wanted. I just wanted to get out of that room. My head was spinning, I felt very nauseous and I was in a lot of pain. My neck was also stiff through being pressed down on the table.

No solicitor was present when I eventually signed the statement. I was not very well educated at that time and my hand was shaking. I could hardly see the paper I was writing on because my head was still pressed against the table. I was finding it difficult to concentrate or even breathe, so a police officer started writing the statement out for me. I couldn't see what he wrote, I just signed it because I knew as soon as I did I'd be able to get up off that table and be placed in a cell. I was desperate for the toilet and I'd gone stiff down one side as I was in so much pain. I just wanted it all to be over, but I was frozen with fear at what the outcome would be.

I was soon taken from the interview room straight over to central detention at Manchester City Courts. I was held for five days along with the Ikegulu brothers, who were also arrested and had made identical statements against me. Kane Clarke decided to hand himself in to a police station after going on the run for five days; he too was brought to central detention in Manchester.

The next morning we were all put in the dock together. I still had no solicitor to represent me and I wasn't offered a duty solicitor. I hadn't slept properly for five days and I was devastated by what had taken place.

CHAPTER FIVE

CRIME AND PUNISHMENT

I was charged with murder, assaulting a police officer and conspiracy to rob. I felt numb, frozen with fear at the outcome of the hearing. Reality had kicked in and I knew I was in serious trouble.

We were all put on remand together and sent to HMP Strangeways, Manchester, until the trial date, which was going to be set for nine months later. Kane and I were led straight to the segregation unit on the lower ground floor, which is the punishment section of the prison. I've since found out it was illegal to place us in there, due to our youth and the fact that we'd committed no infractions of prison rules. The Ikegulu brothers were placed in the main prison on various wings.

Kane was placed into one of the first units. I was told to

walk along the tiled floor near the wall in a straight line, and not to step on the outer floor area. One of the screws was aggressive and had a resentful tone in his voice. The rules they had created pressured and humiliated inmates like myself and seemed to amuse them, for example not allowing any prisoner entering the segregation unit to walk across the main floor. Their two-tiled perimeter walk made it quite awkward.

I knew there and then, with the aggression with which the screws were treating me, life was going to be very difficult for me. I felt frightened at what lay ahead, but at the same time I thought if that was the way things were going to be, I'd have to stand up for myself and fight back.

Of course I knew I'd done wrong and I'd hold my hands up to what was in store for me as punishment. But I refused to be used as a punchbag and deprived of my human rights or dignity. I was not prepared to put my head in the sand and crumble; I had to stand my ground even though I knew the odds were stacked against me. But I was anxious at the prospect of a life in prison, especially when I knew that the regime was operating as a law unto itself.

The first night in the segregation unit was horrendous, it was dark and cold and very noisy. It was hard to sleep but I knew I was in prison now for the long haul. I had to adapt to the situation and just get on with it. After a few days I was placed in a cell on E-wing, the remand section, but it wasn't long before I was put back down into segregation for six months. The segregation unit is a punishment block where your privileges are taken from you and you are segregated from other inmates. Sometimes it can lead to harsher measures, such as restraint in a body belt if you don't comply with their made-up rules and regulations. I would not comply or put up with their brutality and verbal abuse. I'd go out of my way to be disruptive because of the way I was treated. I was in the seg unit from day one because of my non-compliance with a regime that mistreated me.

I found it easier to cope by being alone, not having to share my personal space with anyone else. I never wanted to double-up in that shithole – although there were days when I felt lonely and sick of walking around in circles.

And I guess I sometimes regretted my actions in fighting the regime, but I was stubborn to a fault. I could have kept my head down like most inmates do, but it's just not me. I wanted to make it clear from the start that they could have it the easy way, by treating me with respect as a human being, or the hard way. I always had it in my head that one day I'd beat the system and come out the better man.

After six months in segregation my punishment time was up. I was taken back up to the remand wing where I kept myself to myself, working out and keeping my mind active with reading and writing. I kept myself out of trouble for the ten weeks leading up to the trial.

The trial started on 6 October 1981, and lasted four days. We were all sentenced together – all five of us mixed-race, with black fathers and white mothers, in front of an all-white jury – even though I had legit representation this time, I didn't have confidence in my defence team. The prosecution had no concrete evidence to prove that it was me who caused Mr

Gilbert's death; there was no blood on my clothes or shoes and the knife only had a speck of blood on the very tip; there were many contradictory police statements but my own confession, even though it was made in horrible circumstances, didn't help me.

It didn't take long for the jury to deliberate their verdict. When the foreman read it out to me it was like someone reading in slow motion:

'Alan Lord, we the jury find you guilty of murder, guilty of assaulting a police officer, and guilty of conspiracy to commit robbery.'

I wanted the floor to open up and swallow me. Even though it was a shock to hear the guilty verdict read out, I was kind of expecting the response – especially after the prosecutor provided the jury with a photo of Mr Gilbert after the pathologist had performed an autopsy. It left a disturbing image of him lying on that autopsy table that will be with me till the day I die.

Still, I'd had to cling onto the hope that the jury would believe I truly had no intention of killing David Gilbert. But it was no good. They had made their deliberation and I was given a life sentence, with a minimum tariff of fifteen years.

As I was led away I felt numb. I was frozen with fear because I knew it was the end for me. I'd already had a taste of prison life and knew exactly what was in store. But I had to compose myself and keep it together because I didn't want to show anyone, especially the other lads, that I was crumbling at the outcome of my sentence.

CHAPTER SIX

STARTING MY SENTENCE

I was taken back to Strangeways, only this time I was not on a remand wing. I was put on the other side of the prison to start my life sentence. The inmates at Strangeways were treated badly most of the time and often locked up for twenty-four hours a day with just enough food to survive on. The food, when it wasn't tasteless, was revolting.

The daily slop-outs are best left to one's imagination – but I'll tell you anyway. The chamber pot or slop bucket was left in your cell and could only be changed once a day, sometimes with three men to a cell. If it was full of excrement or overflowing, you could ring the bell and one inmate would be allowed to take it to the only toilet at the end of the wing and slop it out. But most of the time the bell was ignored, or sometimes they would make excuses not to allow the inmates to change the pot or bucket, like not having enough staff working on that shift. So the stench would stay in the cell overnight until the morning, when inmates lined up along the wing with their buckets overflowing.

After serving five months in Strangeways, which felt like five years, I was moved to Wakefield Prison in Yorkshire. I was placed on B-wing but it wasn't long before I was taken down to the segregation unit, where I was locked away without privileges for twenty-four hours a day. I wasn't going to take any of their verbal abuse and gave them as much back as they were dishing out to me.

I was young and rebellious and didn't want anything from them that they could take back from me, which included everything in my cell. I took out the bed, the locker and anything else I could remove and threw it over the railings onto the wire mesh. All I ever had in my cell was a sheet to cover myself while I slept on the floor, and my toiletries were neatly packed away in case of a sudden move. That was the way it would be for me throughout my entire imprisonment.

It took me a long time to realise that all the conflict and fighting against the regime had achieved nothing for me. It only got me placed in the segregation unit, the punishment suite, the block, the cage, and all the time it was just a game to them. I was taunted and wound up with their derogatory comments and brutality. Just to get a slight reaction from me would be seen as a victory by a warped screw, but sometimes it backfired and one of the screws would come off worse – or the prison would have me shipped out. It took me years to understand that the segregation unit was exactly where they wanted me. I'd become a nuisance to the regime and was eventually listed as Britain's twenty-third most dangerous prisoner by the Home Office. The truth is that I'm no more dangerous than anyone else in society, and eventually I'll prove it.

There were around 800 prisoners in Wakefield and only 210 were not sex offenders. The locals called the prison 'the Monster Mansion'.

One time, I was in my cell when one of the lads came in and told me that some nonce, as we called paedophiles, wanted the channel of the television in the communal room turned over and had gone to complain to a screw. I went down to the television room and shouted to the screw, telling him the nonce was not dictating what could be watched. I got verbal because I was sick of nonces getting their own way and having preferential treatment. The screw knew we were right and didn't change the television's channel.

But the next morning I was sent to the segregation unit. I got the blame for disruption, as usual, even though the dispute had already started before I got to the television room.

I was placed in the segregation unit for seven days; I guess it was my strong mind and my will to survive that got me through. Since I started my sentence in the segregation unit, I didn't feel the difference when the regime was trying to punish me by placing me in there. I had no possessions for them to take; I wasn't bothered about having any contact with other inmates because I knew I'd be moved around from prison to prison. That was my way of survival within the system.

I spent eighteen months in Wakefield. I hated each and every day that I spent in there, being among the paedophiles made my skin crawl. I wasn't sharing the same wing, but the thought of how many child-sex offenders there were in there made me want to get out as soon as possible. I wanted to cause problems to get shipped out.

The screws' training college was adjacent to the prison, and those who were on their probation period were assigned to duty on the segregation unit. The macho attitude that they brought into the unit with them was encouraged by those permanently assigned there. To me they were absolute cowards who could only operate in a group. Strangely enough, some of the screws were ex-miners, working-class socialists who had been made redundant from disused collieries at Salford or Bradford.

I remember when I returned to the wing from the segregation unit, I was placed in a different cell. I think they just wanted to watch me throw everything out of my cell again and cause a disturbance so I'd be marched back to segregation. I was so pissed off with them that I barricaded myself in there for eighteen hours. I put everything I could behind the door – the wardrobe, bed, table and chair – and smashed everything up. I put a damp cloth over my mouth, then put boot polish all over the walls and set it on fire. I was so mad with the way I was being treated that I just wanted to cause as many problems for that dirty prison as possible, so they'd move me out. This time it didn't work and I was moved to another cell. So I threw everything out and started with my cleaning ritual...

Another time I heard a lot of commotion and went downstairs to find out what was going on. One of the officers was taking all the commission off the lads from their mail-order catalogues. I started arguing with a senior officer who was sticking up for the screw who was taking advantage. There was a group of lads stood around my friend Joe from Liverpool. I liked Joe, I had a lot of respect for him and he was like a father figure to me. He told me to leave it because he knew what I was like; I wouldn't have any screws taking liberties with inmates, especially my friends. Joe tried to defuse the situation and some of the lads started dispersing. Then I saw a screw laughing at me.

'Keep laughing and see what happens!' I told him.

Joe had gone back upstairs and I started walking towards my cell, but when I looked back the screw still had a smile on his face. I turned back, walked over and whacked him on the chin, knocking him to the floor. I soon took the smile off his face.

But I had a feeling things were not going to go smoothly and there was going to be a backlash. A few minutes later the riot alarm went off and everyone had to go to their cells. The screws started running through the wings, making sure prisoners were locked down.

I was brushing my teeth when I heard a noise at my door. A screw named McCall was stood outside my cell with some others.

'Your name has been given to me as the instigator of the incident downstairs, Lord. Come out of your cell now, you're going down to the seg unit,' he said aggressively.

Wiping my mouth, I walked out of my cell. Little did McCall know that I still had toothpaste in my mouth; as I got to the door I spat it right into his face. He and some other screws grabbed hold of me and I was frogmarched down to the segregation unit.

I wasn't in seg for long, about eight days; I remember it well because I spent my twenty-first birthday down there. I was put back on normal location but it didn't last long before I was in trouble again, this time for punching a sex offender in the face. The dirty nonce shouldn't have said something under his breath when he was walking past me.

Naturally, I just wanted out of Wakefield, and I soon got my chance when fires were being started in some of the paedophiles' cells – unfortunately while they were outside.

There were several cells set alight. It was obvious no one would own up to starting the fires, so we were all sent down to the segregation unit in groups. I was in the second line-up to be taken down to seg, but the fires were still taking place. I guess it was a bit like *Spartacus* – all the non-sex offenders stood up for one another regardless of who was starting the fires.

I was sent to the strip cell. I needed to do something else to get out of that prison so I started banging on the walls and ripping the tiles up off the floor. I didn't get much sleep that night, as I knew I'd probably also get blamed for the fires. The next morning the cell door opened and a senior screw threw some clothes at me, telling me to get dressed immediately because I was being moved out.

So I told the screw I was not going to comply with his

demand until he spoke to me properly. He just carried on calling me a black bastard and mimicking monkey noises. As I stepped out of the cell I picked up my chamber pot. In those days screws were not provided with protective clothing so they backed off from me, knowing they could be covered in piss and shit.

The senior screw told one of the others to grab hold of me. A fat screw came towards me and I threw the contents in his face. He ran at me and pushed me to the floor; they all started piling into me. One of them had my leg twisted over his leg backwards, trying to damage my kneecap. It didn't work so he got out his truncheon and started whacking my toes.

Even though it really hurt I didn't show it. I just gritted my teeth. I had no chance of any kind of movement because there were too many of them holding me down. Eventually they put me in a body belt, carried me up the stairs and threw me into a room where the governor was waiting for me.

'I am moving you, Lord, on a section 1074.'

'What's a 1074?' I asked. In fact it's a good behaviour report.

'I do not have to tell you anything, Lord...'

Then three or four screws dragged me outside and threw me onto the floor of a waiting van. They jumped in and started trampling all over me. I was in the van for a couple of hours and the brutality was ongoing.

When the van finally stopped they dragged me out; my feet didn't even touch the floor. I saw a sign for Durham prison. I was taken straight down to the segregation unit on

45

A-wing; they threw me into the strong box, a cell within a cell they call 'the cage'. I stood up but they threw me to the floor and restrained me in a figure-four position. Then they took the body belt off me and backed off.

I stood up and brushed myself down. I wasn't going to let them break me. I'd got my way in the end, because I was out of Wakefield, out of the Monster Mansion. Although it was a pretty rough landing it was worth it to be out of that shithole.

It was the back end of 1982 when I gracefully arrived at Durham prison. I felt like a caged animal; I was in a lot of pain from my violent ride over. I could barely hold my arms out and could only just stand up inside the cage, where there was only a mattress.

I was only in there a few minutes when I heard a knock on the wall. I went to the window and the inmate in the next cell explained he'd been sent down to the seg unit for doing the governor in. He told me he'd whacked him in the mouth and fought with some of the screws.

He asked me if I wanted to go for them when they opened the door, and like a fool I said yes. I was getting myself involved again, but that was me – never one to turn down a good go at the system.

I waited for a while until my door opened, and there stood the biggest screw I'd ever seen in my life. He was around six-foot four inches tall and built like a brick shit-house. It was obvious they'd sent him down as a way of letting me know not to mess with their prison. I'd been sent to Durham under a controlled restraint and they thought they'd try to intimidate me by sending this big man, whose name was Lurch.

The screw walked into my cell and poked his finger down hard on the desk.

'While you are in here, Lord, you will comply with the rules. You think you are some kind of hard man, don't you – a big-time weightlifter?'

I knew he was going to be trouble, I could tell by the way he was staring at me. Then something came into my head: *I am going to punch your big fat face in.*

As he exited after his lecture, I looked round the cell to see what I could find to whack him with. I noticed some old red-and-white light bulbs; I took them out and hid them behind the mattress.

After a couple of hours the big screw came back and opened the door. He had a tray of food in his hand; he stretched out with his keys still in the lock and asked me if I wanted something to eat. He had a smirk on his face as if he'd done something to the food.

I had the light bulbs in my hands behind my back. I moved slightly to one side. The bulbs knocked together and made a noise. He realised I had something in my hands and looked at me as if to question it.

Then I threw one of the bulbs to one side and ran at him. He turned round to get out of the door. I pushed him with all my bodyweight, knocking him to the ground. He went straight down and curled up into a ball. I shouted at him: 'Don't ever fucking talk to me again like I'm some kind of fucking idiot, and don't treat me like I'm a fucking animal!'

I started hitting him on the head and he squealed like a pig. I put the light bulb into his ear and dug it inside as far as I could, twisting it round until it crunched. I saw another screw come to the door and look through in shock. He didn't intervene because he must have thought if I could take Lurch down he needed more backup.

The next minute there were several screws on me. They came in their numbers, kicking and using their truncheons, beating me all over. They restrained me by sitting on me and twisting my legs up my back. At one point they were falling all over each other.

I was put back into the body belt, a medieval contraption consisting of a thick leather belt about three inches wide, with two heavy metal ratchets on the front and two on the back. They tightened it to the last notch, even though they knew it was hard to breathe at that point. My hands were positioned with one tied to the front and one tied to the back. My shoulders were almost dislodged.

While I was in the belt they laid me flat on the floor. The big screw I attacked earlier knelt down and put a knife to my neck.

'If the governor wasn't here I'd cut your fucking throat, you black bastard!'

I knew he was serious when I looked up and saw his eyes bulging out of his head. I could also see a man in a suit to the side of me, and only governors wore suits in those days. Then Lurch stuck the knife deep in my arm and sliced it. I have a nice scar as a permanent souvenir; another memento for me to look back on.

After lying on the floor for a while, I must have dozed off. I was then woken by hundreds of roaches; they were crawling all over me, the walls and the floor. I jumped up and started brushing them off, jumping round the cell like a Red Indian. The screws heard the noise and came back for me; I was dragged out and lifted into the air. The prison was on lockdown as they took me to D-wing, in the old part of the prison. I was thrown on the floor in a strip cell and left there overnight.

The following morning the door was slung open. Several screws stood there, chanting monkey sounds and walking around like apes. One said, 'Throw the black bastard a banana!'

I didn't have any clothes on for all of the seven days I was there; I was not given much to eat either, just scraps thrown in on the floor. I was very weak and drained. After seven days black eyes and bruises generally clear up, leaving no trace of the previous violence, and unsurprisingly it was only then that I was allowed out.

The body belt was tightened to the last notch so that my shoulder was in constant pain. It was frozen stiff after a few days and I found it very difficult to move. On the fifth day a couple of screws opened the door and stood staring at me. I could see one of them had something for me to eat; they took it in turns to spit in the food, and the screw holding it threw it into a puddle of urine that had resulted from me not being able to move.

I wanted to demonstrate how I was going to survive regardless of their inhumane treatment, so I started eating

49

the food like a dog, licking every bit off the floor. They were all laughing and chanting at me, barking like dogs. I guess I kept them amused before they finished their shift and went home to their sad lives. It was something for them to brag about in the pub.

Technically, they are not supposed to keep you in the body belt if you are not 'refractory' (violent towards them) – which I was not. They are also supposed to check on you every hour, which they did not, and to take you out of the body belt and out of the cage.

Contrary to the rules and regulations, I was kept in the body belt for seven days. It was very degrading and humiliating to be placed in that situation, and if it had been someone else without a strong will to survive, I think it would have made them go crazy.

The Independent Monitoring Board is supposed to monitor the situation but they are incredibly ineffective. It seems impossible that they couldn't know that prisoners are mistreated and that brutality takes place behind closed doors; they must know that the screws make up their own rules and punishments, but nothing ever seems to get done. I doubt it will change in the future. There is always bound to be a storm brewing somewhere in one of our prisons.

At the end of the seven days I spent in the cage, the governor came to my cell door and lifted the Judas hole.

'We don't want you in our prison, Lord; you're being moved out today.'

That was all he had to say. The screws took me out of the cell. I was still in the body belt and naked, they escorted me to the reception area just as I was, stinking and cold. I must have looked a terrible mess. I'd only lasted eight days in Durham Prison and I was happy to see the back of it.

I was put in the waiting van. It was very cold because it was winter and had been snowing. I was freezing and felt very weak after eating very little for over a week. I didn't know where I was going but it felt like I was travelling for a long time. When I got to the prison gates and the door was opened I realised I was at Gartree Prison in Leicester.

Even though I was still in a body belt, I was taken to the reception area to go through the routine of checking in and having my ID photo taken. I asked the reception officer if there were any sex offenders in their prison.

'No, we don't have them here, Lordy; they are all straight lads in here.'

Even though I was in a state I knew things could only change for the better. The prison did not look that bad. I was given clean clothes and taken to the showers, after being taken out of the body belt. But I felt as stiff as a board. I could hardly walk properly for days and couldn't sleep on my left side because my arm was still in a lot of pain.

CHAPTER SEVEN

TRYING TO SETTLE DOWN

Gartree was not that bad for a dispersal prison – a big Cat A jail that holds prisoners with lengthy or life sentences. Although there were two small riots and disturbances before I got there, my time in Gartree went smoothly. I just got on with my weight training and tried to stay out of trouble, I filled my days with writing and reading, always got my head down very early and got up early for circuit training. But after my being there for around eighteen months and settling into some kind of routine, it all kicked off with a black feller called Walker and a screw.

It all started when a dog handler came to work on my landing. He was a bit of a shithead and walked around like he was ten men. It was early one morning and I was in the shower after my morning workout. This screw went past the showers and got drenched from head to toe. I knew by the smell and the look on his face that someone had thrown their slop bucket over him. When Walker went past me with his coat on I knew it was him who'd thrown the bucket. There was another black feller, called Garrett, who stood there laughing at the screw as he rushed to get off the landing. I found out later that another screw saw Garrett laughing and pressed the riot button.

There was no need for that. There was no disturbance or conflict going on, no protest or even any loud verbals. It was just someone who found it funny to see a screw with a chewed-up face stinking of piss, rushing to get out of his stinking clothes.

One of the things I liked about Gartree Prison was the unity between the inmates. We were always watching out for each other and stood by if there was any trouble. So when some of the lads heard the riot bell go off they jumped out of their beds to see where the trouble was.

I was still in the shower at this point but came running down the landing naked to see what was going on. I was covered in soapsuds and slipping all over the place; I must have looked like a snowman.

And I could clearly see Garrett on the floor with several screws holding him down, trying to restrain him. I ran over to one of them and whacked him in the face. As I had nothing on and couldn't get a grip, I ran back to the shower, washed the soap off and got dried. I ran to my cell, put my gym gear on and went running back on the landing.

By this time there were more inmates shouting for the

screws to lay off Garrett. I picked up the squeeze mop, snapped it in half and went over to the screws with the stick. I punched one bearded screw in the jaw.

'What was that for?' he said.

'You know what that was for,' I replied.

I turned round and saw a bunch of screws holding back. They had seen me coming towards them with the sticks and run off down the wing. I got them in the corner and started whacking them. They were climbing all over each other to escape the blows like the Keystone Kops. I think they were scared because I must have come across as a madman, but I was fully aware of what I was doing. I just wanted to give them a taste of their own medicine.

This went on for a minute or two, and then I felt someone jump on my back. It was David Fraser, son of the gangster Mad Frankie Fraser.

'That's enough, Al, leave it mate, leave it!'

But he may as well have been on the back of an elephant because I finished doing what I had to do – giving the screws a good hiding, just like they were dishing out.

The confrontation on the landing had started to disperse and most inmates were returning to their cells. I threw the sticks to the floor and sat and waited. I knew the riot squad were going to come for me, it was inevitable, and shortly afterwards I heard many footsteps banging down heavily on the landing. The next minute there was a senior screw at my cell door.

'We are here to take you to the seg unit, Lord. We do not want any trouble, so come on out now.'

I picked up a large cotton reel I was using for an art project. It had a chip on the end of it. As I walked towards the cell door I picked the reel up fast and threw it with force at the screw's face, cutting him on his head. He immediately went back out of the cell and slammed the door shut.

It was not long before some screws came back and piled in. We were fighting for about eight or nine minutes, but eventually they got the better of me. They carried on beating me for several minutes; I was fighting back but outnumbered, as usual. They would let me get up and then knock me back down – but to me that just separated the man from the mouse.

They restrained me, took me to the new segregation unit and threw me in a padded cell. I went into the cell because I didn't want to give them the satisfaction of kicking the shit out of me again.

When I was in the cell, I sat there all day thinking of what I could do to get back at them. I don't know why but it crossed my mind to run at the walls, to see if I could get hold of the padding with my teeth and rip it. I finally got my teeth stuck into the padding. I was chuffed that I'd found a way to get back at them and spent about an hour ripping the padding apart.

I then started kicking the door with full force. The next minute, some screws opened the door and came rushing in to restrain me. But this time, one of them kicked me hard in the testicles and jumped on my stomach before they put me in a body belt. They made sure the belt was as tight as possible, but made a mistake by not tying my feet together. As soon as they went out of my cell, I got on the floor on my back and started kicking the door again.

Eventually the screws came back in the cell, grabbed hold of the belt around my stomach and threw me against the wall, punching me several times in the head. Then they told me I was being transferred.

They escorted me out of the prison naked, except for a body belt. There were some women from the board of visitors standing near the entrance where the van was waiting for me. I shook my penis from side to side and shouted across to them: 'What do you think of that then, girls, eh?'

The women dropped their heads down in embarrassment. I was pushed into the van and taken to Winson Green Prison in Birmingham. The screws that took me made it quite clear I was going to get what was coming to me.

Winson Green was notorious for violence. An inmate had recently been killed and the prison was under investigation. It worked in my favour because I knew they had to be careful about inmates' treatment while the investigation was going on.

I arrived at Birmingham and went to the check-in area. I was asked by the officer in charge if I'd restrain myself from assaulting any of his officers if he took the belt off of me.

'I do not make promises, especially to screws,' I told him.

'Well, you'll have to stay in the body belt then.'

The screw who had escorted me to Birmingham, whom I'd punched in the jaw back at Gartree, said to the screw in charge, 'I wouldn't take that belt off him if I was you, he's a very violent piece of shit.'

So I was taken to a cell and left there for hours.

Sat there in the dark, I was getting more and more agitated at being left to starve in the body belt. I was thinking of how I could get back at them. As the evening wore on, I noticed a rubber stopper on the end of the bed frame. I took it off and used the ratchet to get out of the body belt. Then one of the screws looked through the spy hole and said: 'The bastard is out of the belt!'

I thought then that they'd send in the cavalry but they left me alone all night. I was tired and hungry but still pissed off with them. I started smashing up the cell and started a dirty protest, covering my body in excrement and using it to write all over the walls.

The following morning the governor came to the cell and opened the spy hole.

'Oh. I see you got out of the body belt,' he remarked.

I immediately stood up and shouted, 'Jimmy Boyle!' and held the body belt up in the air. The governor started laughing. Boyle is a Scottish ex-con, the first man who ever got out of a body belt. He shouted, 'Freedom!' when he got loose, so I was mimicking him.

One of the hospital staff looked through the hole and said, 'I see you can spell, Alan,' regarding my writing with the excrement that I'd deposited all over the walls. I do feel a little bit embarrassed when I talk about my dirty protests, because I'm otherwise a very clean person. I've always maintained a high level of hygiene.

The body belt was taken out of my cell and I was taken to the showers, given clean clothes and breakfast. I'd calmed down by the time the governor came to give me my early morning wake-up call. Then I was put in another cell and got my head down – after I threw everything out, of course.

To be honest, even though Birmingham Prison has a very bad reputation I didn't feel threatened. It was not that bad; they were laidback with me and I got to shower every day. The only problem I had with Winson Green was that some days I was locked up for twenty-four hours, whereas the norm was twenty-three, with an hour for exercise, depending on the elements outside. There was no gym or recreation programme and all I could do was pace up and down, trying to use what little space I had to exercise.

Eventually I calmed down after my initial outburst. A few days later, another inmate was brought down to the seg unit, Robson ('Robbo') from Gartree prison. I was put there on GOAD (good order and discipline) for the incident in Gartree, but the screws were alright with us. In the summer months we used to take the windows out of our cells so we could put our legs out and get some sunshine. Most of the day was spent talking through the windows to each other; there was not much else we could do really.

I was in the seg unit for fifty-six days, but it was not that bad because there were two scouser screws down there who were alright with Robbo and I. I guess they just didn't want any trouble, preferring their days to be peaceful without any hiccups or disturbances. They had a cooker and often made stews for us. Some of the screws I met along the way showed respect because they knew I was given a hard time and was only standing up for myself. But most were power crazy and got a kick out of winding me up with their abuse and bullying tactics. They just wanted to see me go into one for their entertainment, or were childish bullies who wanted to say to their mates they had stuck the boot into Alan Lord.

Winson Green was only a local prison so I knew it wouldn't be long before I got moved. I was told that I was heading for Frankland Prison in Durham, but when they came to take me they dropped me off at Strangeways. It was an overnight stop about which I was fuming, because of the previous treatment I'd received there. As soon as I got there one of the screws started smirking at me.

'Oh, you're back are you, Lord?'

But it was short-lived because I was out of there the next morning and taken to Durham Prison for four days. It felt like they couldn't find a prison that would accept me because of my behaviour. I'd become a nuisance because I wouldn't back down from their inhumane treatment and stood up for what I believed in. I wasn't just doing it for myself but for all the other inmates that had to suffer at the hands of a Victorian regime with its arbitrary rules.

When I arrived at Durham Prison I was checked in and taken to a cell. Just before it was opened I noticed an inmate's card on the cell door. It had his name and his time on it, which was only two months. I told the screw I wasn't sharing a cell with anyone. I put the bag with my toiletries in over my shoulder and started walking towards the segregation unit. The screw asked me what I was doing.

'I am not doubling up in a cell with anyone, especially someone who's doing a two-month stint,' I told him.

I'd never had to double up with anyone in the past and I

wasn't going to start now. I walked to the segregation unit on A-wing, having been down there before.

'Where do you think you're going?' called out another screw.

'I'm going into the seg unit, why?' I replied.

'You cannot put yourself in the seg unit.'

'Well I am, so just get on with it.'

They knew I wouldn't back down and would cause them more trouble than it was worth, so they put me in a cell on the second landing. I was still on GOAD on my own, in my own cell.

Really I was so pissed off with them messing me about, taking me from one prison to another, treating me like a piece of dirt, putting me in a shared cell with someone who'd be out in under eight weeks. I was also pissed off with the fact that I'd been taken to Strangeways Prison for a night stop that was unnecessary, so as soon as the cell door closed I started smashing it up.

I wanted out of Durham Prison as soon as possible. I didn't want to stay there for days on end just so they could piss me off. I was not going to let them humiliate me any longer.

Because I knew that there would be trouble, I stripped off my clothes and put all my things together ready for the move. But when they did come for me I didn't expect the level of violence I received.

I tried to fight back but there were just too many of them. They jumped on me and put me in the body belt, picking me up and carrying me down the landing. It took me by surprise that they should beat me at the same time as raising me into the air. When they reached the stairs on the landing they just threw me down them. The stairs at Durham were at a 45-degree angle, so I think their intention was to seriously injure me. I bounced from railing to railing and then hit the stairs hard, rolling down to the bottom. There were other screws stood laughing at me. I still had the body belt on so I couldn't protect myself from the fall or the blows. I think if it hadn't been for the weight I was carrying or the muscle that protected me, I wouldn't be here – or at least I'd be in a wheelchair.

The screws grabbed hold of me and dragged me out to a strip cell on D-wing. They knocked me about for a while until I was nearly unconscious, then undid the body belt and backed out one by one – even though I was so badly beaten that I could hardly see or move my body an inch. I collapsed into a deep sleep and stayed there for what seemed to be days.

When I finally got some strength back and could see out of my almost closed eyes, I decided to go on a dirty protest again. Even though I was still in a lot of pain and finding it hard to move around, I managed to block out the spy hole so no one could see me. Then I started dirtying the cell walls.

I couldn't sleep with the pain in my back and shoulders, so I carried on making a mess all night. I felt very low and degraded as a human being, worthless with very little self-esteem. I felt defeated. But I sat up all night thinking that I must be strong and fight back, because I didn't want them to weaken me and get the better of me, or even to think that they had.

The next morning, the door opened and, to my surprise,

the governor was sat outside my cell behind a table. He had brought a chief officer with him plus several screws each side of him. He conducted the adjudication from outside my cell. I think he must have wondered what the hell had happened to me, as when the cell door first opened the look on his face was of pure horror. But he remained stern.

'I do not want you in my prison, Lord. You are out of here today, understood?' he said.

He got up and the door was closed in my face. I didn't go anywhere until the following day; I was left in the cell with nothing to eat or drink until the next morning, when they came for me. I was still naked and covered in my excrement, as I had been for two days. I was taken down to the showers and thrown some clothes, ready for my move.

CHAPTER EIGHT

FOUR YEARS IN FRANKLAND

I was taken into a waiting van early that morning and driven to Frankland prison, Durham. I found it very strange that I'd been on a diversion for six days. When I arrived at Frankland they were very surprised to see me in such a state.

'Why was he not brought here last week? He should have been here a week ago,' said one of them.

'Nothing to do wi' me,' said another. 'Take it up with the governor.'

That just proved to me that they were holding on to me to give me a hard time.

I was in Frankland Prison for four years. Frankland is a dispersal prison. I was put on D-wing, next to the gym. There were only eighteen nonces in Frankland and they were confined to a landing on a wing. The sex offenders would never be allowed to mix with other prisoners, and rightly so.

Then I started working. My first job was in the furniture shop and then I went on the garden party. At first I didn't think I'd get the garden job, as I'd already tried to escape and been caught. But I think they wanted to break my pattern of behaviour and give me a chance to prove I could be trusted.

But to my surprise I got the job on the garden party and started working outside with the plants and the trees. I really enjoyed it and got on well with the lads I was working with. Everyone looked out for each other in Frankland prison. I used to go round collecting the plants from the administration offices to take them to be watered, only some of them never made it back and ended up on my wing in the quiet room, as did a nice big chair that had been made in the woodwork shop. We made the quiet room cosy and had a laugh while doing it up; we were always adding something to it.

Time seemed to pass without too many disturbances. I guess I'd got my head around my sentence and adjusted to my surroundings on a daily basis. The four seasons came and went. I found that if I kept my head down and got on with my daily routine of fitness, fresh air and food, I was alright. Time just moved on. I was never one to watch time or cross off a calendar; I never watched television or listened to the radio, so I never knew what was going on outside the prison walls, in the real world. I still had nothing in my cell, only my sheet on the floor and my toiletries. I was always on a personal protest against the regime and found it easier to get through the day knowing they could not take anything else away from me; they had already taken my liberty.

I didn't even read newspapers. It stayed that way throughout all my time in prison; I guess it was just the way I wanted to get through my time. But I'll never forget the Chernobyl nuclear incident, in Ukraine. I found out about the leak because, a few weeks after the incident, we started getting lamb chops on the prison menu for quite a long time. I found it very strange because we'd never had chops inside Frankland before. It was acknowledged soon after that a radioactive cloud had drifted across to Britain and radiation was detected in Wales; as a result, thousands of lambs were slaughtered, hence the prison ending up with 'Chernobyl Chops'. It prompted my suspicions that maybe we were being used as guinea pigs. So Chernobyl Chops were right off my menu, and my dizzy spell and bulging stomach that accompanied them soon went away. I remember telling some of the lads we wouldn't need light bulbs in there soon, because we were going to light up in the dark – that's if we didn't explode first.

Even though I was in Frankland for four years, the only time I ended up in the segregation unit was when I took a small piece of wood from the garden to give to an inmate who wanted to make a new perch for his birdcage. I went to the gym and put the stick in my pocket to pass to my mate; when I was walking back to my cell, I was stopped by a screw I didn't recognise.

When he asked me what was in my pocket, I replied, 'It's a small stick, why?'

'You cannot have that,' he said.

I didn't want to get into any verbals with him and I knew I could get another piece of wood for my mate, so I took the stick out of my pocket and gave it to him. But I told him to go use it on his wife when he got home as a vibrator, and called him a controlling knobhead.

Of course I know I shouldn't have said that about his wife but he was so smug and full of himself. I knew I'd be punished for it and the next day I was put on disciplinary hearing before the governor, who was a real twat with certain people and used to call everyone 'plastic gangsters'. He didn't like me; I could just tell by the way he looked whenever he passed me. I think he'd been waiting for a long time for me to step out of line.

At the disciplinary the governor asked me if I had my F11, which is a form you get in the segregation unit. I didn't answer. He asked me my name and number. I didn't answer. I used to say to everyone who asked that, 'You know who I am and you know my number – otherwise you're admitting to me that you don't know who you have in your prison.'

He read out the charge and I pleaded guilty. I told the governor I should not have said anything about the screw's wife, and I apologised for that.

'But I'm not apologising for anything else I said.'

The outcome was that I lost my privileges and stayed in the segregation unit for seven days. But in reality I didn't have any privileges to lose, as I had nothing for them to take and I was used to being in the seg unit anyway.

After the week was up I went back on normal location and back to my routine until my time came to move on. I was called to the office and told I was going on a 'progressive move' because of the way I'd behaved in Frankland, keeping my head down and working within the prison. I was a bit gutted because I was so used to Frankland. I liked my job and the lads in there too, but I knew the day had come for me to move on.

CHAPTER NINE

PROGRESSION

I was shipped out to Garth Prison in Preston, Lancashire, and downgraded to Cat-B. This meant less security, no dogs and cameras watching my every move. But I only lasted eight weeks in Garth. I just couldn't settle in.

It was Christmas and I didn't want to be banged up all of Christmas Day. I was walking up and down outside the office and told the screws I refused to be locked down from early morning to lunchtime. They must have thought I was mad, but I wanted to let them know I was protesting about prisoners being banged up on Christmas Day. I'm not religious but there were prisoners in there that were, and some also had small children that they were not going to see on Christmas Day. Some kind of recreational activities would have passed the time for them. I just thought it was wrong that the screws could have their little get together while we were on lockdown, so I started protesting to get the lads out of their cells.

Madeline Malden, the female governor, asked me to come and talk to her in the office. I think they knew I was going to kick off and wanted to defuse the situation, because at the end of the day it was also Christmas for the screws. She asked me to sit down and tell her what my concerns were. She listened to what I had to say; we talked for quite a while and I think she understood where I was coming from. I also told her I didn't like her prison and the way the inmates were treated. The food was disgusting; the portions were not enough to feed a child, let alone a grown man. Some of the screws were on a power trip and were talking down to us. Complaints were seemingly ignored when inmates made allegations that they were being mistreated or slapped around. Prisoners also went without medical attention when they needed it. It was inhumane.

Ms Malden was alright with me but didn't agree with my views, naturally, and said she'd see what she could do but wouldn't promise anything. I thought to myself, *right, stay calm for now and see what happens*.

She said she had to do her landing rounds and asked me if I wanted to walk round with her. I guess it was her way of calming me down. I agreed to go with her. She asked me where my cell was, and when I showed her she was shocked to see I had nothing in it. She told me she used to be a nun and, even though she was in a convent and was not allowed to have material things in her room, she'd had more in her room than I did. I told her I'd always lived that way. I didn't want anything from the regime so they couldn't take anything from me, and that was the way I lived my life.

The outcome of that Christmas was that we were not locked up and were able to spend the day out of our cells.

I wasn't happy being there but I just got on with it; I even started a pottery class to fill in the time, but it didn't work. I hated the place; the treatment was despicable; some of the screws running the place were power-crazy.

The difference between a local medium-security prison and a maximum-security dispersal prison is that in dispersal, lifers and long-term inmates are not getting out for a long while. Things run more smoothly and the lads are left to get on with it. But the local prisons are for prisoners on their way out, moving down the categories getting ready to be released, or for short-term prisoners. The screws know that and some try to make life difficult. The inmates have to be on good behaviour and it's a case of put up or shut up with the daily abuse, or else be moved further from the gate to freedom. They know that at the drop of a hat they can have you sent backwards and ruin any chance of parole.

After a few weeks I'd had enough and wanted to find a way to escape. I came up with an idea and started working in the woodwork department. After a short period I was able to get a hacksaw blade out; I told the teacher in charge I needed a new blade but, before I let him see me throw the old one away, I snapped some off the end so he couldn't see how long the blade was. I did this several times.

I eventually got a new blade out and took it back to my cell. I started sawing through the bars; it took me around two months just to get halfway through. I had to keep painting the bars the same colour and hiding the blades behind the old light fittings in my cell.

Then one day the screws came into my cell to do a search. There was a screw I didn't recognise who was having a good look around; my heart was in my mouth and I was just hoping he didn't find the blades. I was stood outside the cell door watching him; he was just about to leave when he looked up at the light fitting.

Oh no, please don't look up there.

My chances of getting out were looking very slim by the time he got a chair and started pulling at the light fitting; then the blades fell out.

'I don't know anything about them,' I said to the screw, 'you *cannot* pin that on me.'

I told him they could have been there before I arrived. He didn't say a word, just went over to the window and started looking at the bars, prodding at them with a miniature penknife he had on his key ring. It wasn't long before the bottom of the bars I'd only just finished filling in started coming away. He looked at me with a big smile on his face as if to say, *you're well sussed out*, then got on his radio and called for assistance.

Then I was taken straight to the seg unit and given a load of verbal by the screws, but I was bang to rights.

'Get in the cell, you black bastard!' this little fat fucker told me.

'Who do you think you're talking to?' I demanded, promising I was going to whack him all over the place if I got my hands on him.

I walked slowly into the cell and the door was slammed. I started kicking the door and banging hard, telling the screw I wanted out of the prison.

About an hour-and-a-half later, one of the governors came down to see me. It was Madeline Malden, who took me in the adjudication room and said they'd found a security breach in my cell. I said it had nothing to do with me and told her not to make allegations against me, then stood up to walk away.

I was escorted back to my cell and started writing a long statement about corrosion in metals, but they called for the officer from the workroom who said that the cuts in the metal were new. I was found guilty of trying to escape and told I was going to be sent back to a secure prison. I told the governor I didn't want to be in her prison anyway and preferred to be elsewhere, no matter where it was.

Then I went back to my cell and started smashing it up. I was so pissed off at getting sussed after months of sawing through the metal bars. After a few hours they sent a big, fat, ugly female screw to try to talk to me.

'What's up, Lordy, why are you doing this and making all this mess?' she asked.

I screamed at her, 'I want out of this prison now, do you understand?'

She just turned round and walked away. About half an hour later several screws came for me.

'You're out of here, Lord,' they told me.

They escorted me to a waiting van. I had no idea where they were taking me to, but when I started seeing signs for Manchester I hoped they weren't taking me back to Strangeways prison. I knew I'd be in for a long night of disputes till they moved me again.

Since being released, the freedom to do the little things, like walking around gardens such as these, has been a real breath of fresh air.

Above: On the roof of Strangeways it was like being out for a few weeks – you could sunbathe or read a book whenever you wanted.

© *John Giles/PA Archive/Press Association Images*

Below: The media and the prison service portrayed us as animals while we were protesting, but all I've ever wanted was a bit of respect from the regime.

© *John Giles/PA Archive/Press Association Images*

Above left: Who is in charge of your prison now? Not you. We are; and we call the shots!

Above right: We all felt terrible that one of the screws, Walter Scott, had a heart attack and died during the start of the riot. But the accusations that there were twenty dead were just malicious lies designed to turn people against us.

Below: I've never said that I shouldn't be punished for what I did. But the years of abuse were truly barbaric, and I'll always fight for prisoners' rights.

I am grateful I've been given a second-chance at life, and also that Anita has given me the opportunity to tell my story so that people will know what life is really like for prisoners, and why there has to be a change.

Above: Enjoying a day out in Blackpool with Anita

Below: A bonding day with Anita.

CHAPTER TEN

BACK TO WHERE I STARTED

I could not believe it when the gates of Strangeways Prison opened. I'd ended up back where I started. I was taken straight to the segregation unit; it was late when I arrived and when I got to my cell there was no drinking water. I rang the bell but no one came. I started kicking at the door and eventually a night screw came down.

'What do you want?' he asked.

I told him.

'Stop kicking the door because you're not getting any water, understand? You'll just have to wait until the morning!'

'Who are you fucking talking to?' I demanded of him.

I told him I needed some water there and then. He laughed at me and shut the hatch.

'I'm fucking coming for you, you bastard!' I shouted

back at him. 'You've had it now, that's it, you've pissed me off!'

I started kicking at the door again, I heard one of the lads down in the seg unit next to me, Dave Judd, shouting, 'Go on, lad, give it to him Al!'

And I think the screw got a bit nervous, because before long there were several more at my door.

'What is your problem, Lordy?'

'I want some water, so open the fucking door now and let me out!'

'If we open the door there's going to be no trouble, is there Lordy?'

'Just open the fucking door now!'

They opened it and backed off, telling me to get some water. The other inmates in the seg unit were at their doors. Dave and a couple of the other lads shouted out, 'If anything happens to him you'll get it!'

I got some water and asked one of the screws where the little fat bastard was hiding. Then I went back in the cell, banged the door shut and got my head down – on the floor, of course.

Next morning I found some matches that had been left in the cell. I put the filthy mattress up against the cell door, and a load of magazines that were also in there, and set it on fire. I wet my T-shirt and wrapped it round my mouth to stop the fumes choking me.

The screws soon came with fire extinguishers and opened the door, dragging me out. I was taken to another cell and they threw me inside. As soon as the door closed behind me

I smashed it up. They would just have to keep moving me from cell to cell.

I'd smashed five cells on one side of the landing before they decided enough was enough and restrained me in a body belt (as well as giving me another good hiding, of course). They always came in numbers; never in all my years of confinement did one single screw try to take me on.

After they got me in the belt, they threw me in a strip cell. About an hour later, a doctor came round to check me over. I heard him say to the screws, 'You need to get him out of there now and out of that body belt.'

I think the doctor was panicking because he could clearly see I was stressed and in a rage, and that the belt had been tied very tight. I guess he didn't want to take responsibility if anything happened to me. I was taken out of the belt right away and placed in another cell.

As soon as the door closed I was off again: smashing up the cell, trying to kick the door down, shouting at them to get me out of their prison. I did not want to spend another night in Strangeways because of what happened to me there in the past. I hated Strangeways with a passion; it was the most inhumane prison I'd been in. As well as being locked up for twenty-three hours a day and slopping out once a day, I now had to wear an escapee uniform made of denim with yellow strips, which was just taking liberties.

Strangeways was a hellhole. A huge cesspit full of hatred and despair, right in the centre of Manchester. The stench of urine made many men sick to their stomach, with only the smell from Boddingtons brewery to disguise it.

No one knew what was going on in there. Only the governor and the screws knew how much brutality and abuse went on behind locked doors.

The line-up every morning of men with their bucketfuls was enough to make even the hardest criminal lightheaded with the stench of stale urine and shit. The toilet door in the recess was only half-size, so other inmates and screws could see you on the loo if you wanted to avoid shitting in your cell and leaving it in your slop bucket for a day or two. We had one toilet per landing with up to fifty inmates queuing up to slop out with buckets that often spilled over. It was disgusting. The urine used to drip over each landing, ending up on your clothes if you didn't get out of the way in time. If you did get covered in other people's piss it was tough, because you were only allowed one change of clothes, one clean towel and one shower each week. Can you imagine the bugs and bacteria in that shithole?

I've been placed in some institutions in my life, but Strangeways was like a concentration camp. No one ever came out of there the way they went in. Infections and other medical complaints were ignored. I believed letters of complaint about the way prisoners were treated were withheld and never sent out to family members or authority figures. Medical notes and prisoners' prescriptions were seemingly ignored and left in a book in the governor's office.

It was a living nightmare that you just had to endure.

I remember how one time a little screw with a moustache kept looking through the Judas hole at me. So one morning, when I got up very early, I heard a noise at my door and saw the little bastard looking through.

'What are you fucking looking at, you prick?' I said to him. 'You fucking ugly bastard, keep on looking at me and I'll come after you.'

I went to see if he was still there and noticed some metal coming slightly away from the Judas hole. I managed to scrape it off with my plastic knife and fork, making the hole bigger until I could get my head through. I looked down the hall and a screw noticed my head popping out. He had a worried look on his face. I told him, 'I'm coming for you and that little bastard with the 'tache.'

A few minutes later several screws came to my cell.

'Give me the metal, Lord,' one of them told me.

'No, you're getting nothing off me. If you want it, come in and get it.'

But after about half an hour of toying with them, I remembered that my sister was coming on a visit within the next few days. So I threw the piece of metal out of the Judas hole. To my surprise they went away, but after an hour the door opened and there were four screws stood there. One of them told me I was being moved to another cell. I didn't want to fight back because of my visit, so I went to the cell and kept my head down for a few days.

On the day of my sister's visit I sat waiting. I rang the bell and asked the screw where my visitor was. I knew Eunice was due to come at 1 pm. He said, 'Be patient, Lord,' and went away.

I was waiting and waiting. I knew she wouldn't let me

down because she only lived round the corner from the prison. It got to 2.40 and I rang the bell again. He got a bit lippy this time.

'We will let you know when your visitor is here. Now shut up and stop ringing the bell!'

'Listen,' I told him, 'you can mess with me because basically I do not give a fuck. But mess with my family and see what happens.'

At 2.45 the door opened and two screws were stood there.

'Your visitor is here, Lord,' the first said.

'There's not going to be any trouble, is there Lord?' the other one asked.

I ignored them and walked past. I was escorted up to the visitor's room where they put me behind glass. Soon after I sat down, Eunice came in with my niece, Natalie, and my nephew, Curtis. My sister had her hands full as the children were very young, and she was now pregnant with Yasmine, her younger daughter.

Eunice asked what had happened to me, because she'd been sat in the waiting room since well before 1 pm. I told her I'd been waiting for her to arrive and she went mad. She said she kept asking where her brother was but the officer had treated her like a piece of shit, giving her excuses.

I'd only been talking to her for fifteen minutes when a screw came over and said, 'Right, time's up.'

'I don't think so,' I told him. 'I'll tell you how this is going to work: I'm staying here with my sister for another fifteen minutes, and then another half-hour on top of that. In fact I'm going to stay here for an hour.'

If he thought he could keep my pregnant sister waiting around with two children, then they could wait for me to have my hour's visit. Then the big screw came over and stood beside me in the cubicle.

'Right, Lord, time is up,' he told me.

I looked at Eunice, not knowing when I was going to see her again. I just saw red. I stood up and butted the screw. I grabbed hold of the wooden seat I was sat on, ripped it off the floor and smashed it over his head.

It all happened in a split second. My sister was shouting at me to stop and calm down. I told her I'd let no one treat her like that.

She was taken out with the children. Then the other screws came into the cubicle and started laying the boot into me. They grabbed me and carried me out to the segregation unit.

I was treated like a piece of shit while I was in there. The only break I got from my cell was when I attended chapel on a Sunday morning, because they had to allow everyone to do so.

I'd say 80 per cent of the inmates who attended chapel were only there to see their mates from other wings. The majority of them were not religious and had never been to church in their lives; it was more of a social gathering. I was only there to catch up with friends and find out what was going on in the prison. It was always the same on a Sunday: the lads used to pass tobacco round, do their swaps and deals, and the priest preached his self-congratulatory bullshit.

CHAPTER ELEVEN

A STORM BREWING

I remember when two inmates, Taylor and Spencer, were brought down to the segregation unit. They were pissed off with what was going on upstairs with some of the screws and their continuous mistreatment of prisoners. We walked around the yard, talking about the conditions within the prison. We made a collective decision to demonstrate our discontent.

The message was soon conveyed to the prisoners on the landings who were also unhappy at the conditions and treatment they had to endure. The abuse was both mental and physical, and the conditions in Strangeways were disgusting.

We just couldn't let the screws continue talking down to prisoners like they were insignificant, a piece of shit off their shoe, undermining and belittling them. Then there was the physical abuse, with the digs and slaps inmates had to put up with; the humiliation of having the slop bucket tipped over the cell just to wind them up; the food being spat in; the screws coming back after their lunch breaks intoxicated because they were allowed to drink alcohol and starting with their derogatory remarks; the lack of time out of the cell if there was even a drop of rain.

The screws had their own rules and regulations about the treatment of prisoners. No action was taken by the authorities and the government, despite all the letters of complaint from prisoners and their families. Their anxiety and anger were ignored, and it was getting closer and closer to boiling point, but all the dignitaries turned a blind eye. It was a time bomb waiting to explode. We had to stand up for our human rights and dignity.

It filtered through the wings that something was going to happen in the chapel the following Sunday morning. Those who didn't want to get involved had the choice not to attend and to stay in their cells.

Even the screws knew something was brewing. They sent a warning to the governor, Brendan O'Friel, but he chose to ignore the signs even though the tensions were running high.

The atmosphere was fuelling tension. But I thought I'd take the chance to have my voice heard. I'd been complaining of mistreatment in various prisons for years but no one was prepared to listen. I thought if we could have a collective demonstration someone might take heed. It had been going on for decades and the regime was getting away with it from one generation to the next.

On Sunday, 1 April 1990, I woke up early. I was hoping the demonstration would take place, because if it wasn't going to happen I was going to have to stage my own to get me out of there. I couldn't stand the place and wanted to be shipped out instead of treated like an animal. Don't get me wrong: the whole prison system is shameful and unjust, but Strangeways was the pit of hell.

Taylor and Spencer had been moved back up to normal location on the wings, so I didn't know what had been planned. I just knew that something was going to happen that day.

Then my cell door opened and a screw came to escort me to the chapel. There was no sign of anything untoward; the inmates that were attending chapel made their way across the yard. But there was a sombre mood amongst the prisoners; you could cut the atmosphere with a knife.

Then I saw Paul Taylor and he gave me the nod. I knew then it was going to kick off. I just didn't know how it was going to start or who would start it. It could have been any one of us at any time. We didn't plan anything specific, but I couldn't wait to see what was going to happen. And if there was going to be a way out for me...

CHAPTER TWELVE

PROTEST IN THE CHAPEL

There were nineteen screws in the chapel that Sunday morning and two priests conducting the service. We had all settled in as the service commenced. The chaplain sermonised on 'The Blessing of the Heart'. Before he'd finished reading, Paul Taylor stood up and walked down the aisle. He took the microphone out of the reverend's hand.

'This man has just talked about the blessing of the heart. Well, what about forgiveness of the heart? You are keeping us all banged up and treating us like animals...'

'Come on son,' said the chaplain, 'give me the microphone, there is no need for all this...'

But then the other inmates stood up and started donning balaclavas. I knew it was going to kick-off big style. It was going to be a very long day.

The reverend tried to take back the microphone from Taylor, but Paul held onto it and shouted out loud: 'Fuck you and your fucking system! Come on, lads, let's go!'

John Spencer came running down the middle aisle with two sticks and started smashing the front of the altar. I could see the screws were all leaving the chapel in a panic. They weren't going to try to take control of the situation.

It all happened very fast. The chaplain and the other priest had left via the vestry. The lads had the run of the place and started smashing it up.

My initial intention was to escape. I had a good chance. I moved towards the back of the chapel where the last two screws were making for the exit. I caught up with one of them and snatched the chain with a bunch of keys from around his waist. He struggled with me at first and tried to pull the chain back off me, but I was stronger. He looked at me with terror in his eyes and then ran out.

I did a U-turn and dog-trotted down the middle of the aisle, to the left-hand side where they normally brought in the young offenders. As I got near the door I saw two other screws. One tried to close the door behind him, but before he could lock it the other screw had to get out. I caught up to him just as he was about to exit, grabbing hold of his collar.

'Go on, you scumbag, get out!'

I gave him a slap in the face and he ran out. The other screw looked grim. As I grabbed hold of him and punched him in the jaw, he didn't even try to fight back. He ran off with the other screw like two headless chickens.

'You're not so hard now, are you? You little bastards!'

I knew then I couldn't escape because that area was blocked. I went back into the chapel, up the middle aisle and up to one of the inmates to give him the bunch of keys.

'Here you go, mate.'

He took off straight away. I then climbed up the scaffolding onto the roof of A-wing. I was the first one up there. After a couple of minutes I could see inmates appearing on the other roofs; they were waving over to me and putting their arms up in the air.

I didn't know what was going on downstairs. All I knew was it was mayhem and chaos. On the roof of A-wing I had to go down on my hands and knees. I was a bit frightened as I'd never been that high up before and didn't want to lose my balance. I took my time, crawling slowly towards the end of the block, but when I got to the first skylight I slipped and put my hand right through it. It cut badly and I had to rip off my shirt to wrap it round my hand tight and stop the blood flow.

I got to the end of the roof and looked down. I could see lots of screws, some governors and other officials. They could see me and some started shouting abuse, threatening to break my arms and legs.

'Who's in charge of your prison now?' I shouted back. 'We have control and we want justice for what you've done to us.'

I felt free as a bird on that roof. I knew I was in deep trouble and would have to spend a longer time in prison, but I was already a lifer and needed to let as many of the press as possible know what was going on in Strangeways, even if it meant sacrificing my own time.

During the twenty-three days of the demonstration I felt a sense of freedom. I lived for each and every moment that I was not confined in a small cell. It was a wonderful feeling. I wanted to demonstrate for as long as we possibly could, in the hope that we could change the prison's punishment system. I'd already served ten-and-a-half years in various prisons, but I thought that if we could get media attention my extra years would not be in vain.

The lads were able to get newspapers because the screws would send them up on a piece of string, I think they wanted us to know how we were being portrayed in the papers. It was through an article in the *Manchester Evening News* that I read about two negotiators, Peter Hancock and David Wriggbey, saying in an interview that the lads on the roof should get at least ten years on top of their sentence for rioting.

While I was on the roof, exchanging verbals with the screws, I realised I'd split my pants. I had to get back down and find a way to the kit-change storeroom, so I climbed down the rotunda, working my way to the locker room. The place was in a mess as inmates were still smashing it up. I found my way through, broke the door open and got changed.

Realisation kicked in that I was in the middle of a serious prison riot. A small protest had clearly got out of hand. There was no sign of the screws being able to restrain us. There was no organised plan put in place for any such disturbance. The inmates were left to run riot. It was a lawless situation and we had taken over the prison.

I found my way back to the roof of A-wing and sat there

awhile, chatting to some of the other lads. I could see crowds of people gathering in the streets outside the prison. There were sirens going off all over the place.

The first few days seemed to go very fast because we were all on an adrenalin high. I couldn't believe how no attempts were made to get us off the roof or round the lads up from down below. There were a vast amount of prisoners who would protest for just a few days. As the days went on, more and more inmates handed themselves in. But it was a surprise that neither the riot squad nor any other force tried to stop the protest.

Throughout the demonstration I took every opportunity to search for materials that could be put to our advantage, to expose the wrongdoing of the prison system. I went back down into the prison – it was a complete mess, it looked like a tornado had passed right through it. I found my way through all the rubble to the governor's office, and found two books full of complaints of great significance to our cause. One book contained prisoners' complaints on withheld letters to family members which they'd never received. The other book concerned the wrong medical treatment or wrong diagnoses of prisoners. Clearly, neither had gone any further than the governor's office.

While I was on the roof, there had been rumours that some sex offenders had been attacked down below in E-wing, and I was also told that part of the prison was on fire. It was mainly the young offenders that were after the dirty nonces. I don't condemn them for giving them what they deserved, but I wasn't interested in any witch hunt. My foremost intention was to escape but it wasn't possible, so I decided to protest for my human rights.

I stayed on the roof most of the time; I only came down to find provisions because I knew we were now in it for the long haul. I also wanted to find evidence of neglect and abuse of prisoners for the media to read. The police had turned on loud music through large microphones from their vans, so we couldn't talk directly to the press about our treatment.

The press were based above solicitor Mary Munson's office across the road from the prison. I was shouting as loud as I could to get our message across and to get the police to turn their ridiculous music off, but it just got louder. They were playing a Barry Manilow song over and over again ('Her Name Was Lola') to drown the shouting from the lads trying to communicate with relatives. As soon as I got the chalkboard and started communicating with the press, the music stopped.

One of the lads from the press who was there from the very first to the last day was taking lots of photos of us. I later found out his name was John Giles and he still works in the media. We'd meet up again some thirty-two years later on a television show for the BBC with governor Brendan O'Friel, called *Reunite*.

I was also able to talk to my mate Billy Gould (RIP), who'd come down to the prison to support me. Billy was a good man who stood up for the human rights of prisoners. He was also a very good boxer and very much into fitness, like myself. I'd met Billy a few years earlier in Wakefield

Prison and we became good friends. I've always carried Billy's advice with me. He was there for days on end at the Strangeways protest because he himself had witnessed just what the prison regime is capable of. Billy was caught up in the Hull Prison riots, which resulted in him having his legs broken in various places by the screws. He was also later charged with conspiracy just for talking to me at the Strangeways Prison protest, but was cleared.

The music was getting louder and louder, and was pissing me off. I went back down to try to find something to write messages on. I managed to get into one of the classrooms and pulled the blackboard off the wall. I found some chalk and went straight back onto the roof to prepare messages for the media.

As I said before, the music soon stopped because I'd found a way of communicating. One of the first messages I wrote was about the injustice committed against Oliver Brady; Ollie was an inmate who'd been wrongly imprisoned and had been contesting his innocence for many years. I met him in Frankland Prison and truly believed he was an innocent man. I remember the police hovering very low in a helicopter over the prison; I held the chalkboard up to them with my message and put the thumbs up. The image was captured by the press.

While we were on the roof there were all kinds of accusations against us, including mass murder and bodies left on the wings. I remember someone shouting up to ask one of the lads if we'd killed any paedophiles. The newspaper headline read: '20 DEAD'.

It was all lies. The police, screws and press caused unnecessary panic to the families of all concerned, to the extent that body bags were brought to the side of the prison walls and a hotline was set up for worried relatives.

The only prisoner that died because of his injuries was a paedophile named Derek White. I heard that he'd abused a little girl and a good beating resulted in his death. I was later charged along with four other inmates for his murder, even though I'd never laid eyes on him. They couldn't pin that one on me because it turned out that he died from a blood clot. 'That means less children will be suffering at the hands of a sex fiend,' was all I could say. I didn't feel sorry for him and I knew no one else in the protest would either. In the trial that was to take place at a later date, it turned out that White was a prolific sex offender, as confirmed by the legal teams. I wasn't there while the attack was taking place and had never seen the nonce, so I didn't have much to say other than that I wasn't involved.

The only other death was a prison officer who died of a heart attack unrelated to the prison protest.

We had to take it in turns to be on watch, because the screws had tried to sneak onto the roof and surround us a few times. It had to be round-the-clock observation. But as some prisoners started to fade and give themselves up, the rest of us started to organise things much better between one another. I tried to advise some of the young offenders to go down and hand themselves in at the start of the protest, because I didn't want them to end up with a long sentence, especially when some of them were inside for joyriding or something petty like that. They had no idea of what was really going on inside the prison system because they hadn't served enough time to find out.

However I didn't regret one day of my twenty-three days on the Strangeways protest. I read the papers to keep up with what the press were saying, and what lies and bullshit the regime was coming out with. But I was very surprised when I read an article about Mrs Susan Gilbert, the wife of the man I was convicted of murdering. To my amazement, Mrs Gilbert spoke out in my defence; she was obviously mentally scarred by what had occurred that day, but still didn't feel that prisoners like me deserved to be treated like animals. I was relieved that she spoke from her experience as a youth worker about how young people could make terrible mistakes.

I became the negotiator and tried to get my voice heard, writing messages on the blackboard for all to see. The first was: 'The sentence justifies the crime but the years don't because it's barbaric.' We kept ourselves busy with banter and camaraderie amongst ourselves, shouting to the press in the warehouses across the way. We also had our families and friends outside, and support from members of the general public with banners protesting the way prisoners were treated in Strangeways.

We wanted to speak about the conditions inside Strangeways. We wanted change to the sanitation, the daily slop-out and weekly shower; we wanted more than one hour out of the overcrowded cells; an improvement on the disgusting food and portions; more communication with relatives; more visits. We wanted to expose the way the regime was running Strangeways, and the harsh punishments and brutality of some of the screws.

One day I went down to the kitchen to sort some provisions out for the lads and couldn't believe what I found. There were huge steaks and hundreds of large chops in the freezer. I found it very strange, as the nearest we ever got to meat was corned beef hash.

On the twenty-third day of the protest there were only six of us left; we were all determined to stay on the roof as long as possible, but at the same time I couldn't understand how six prisoners were allowed to demonstrate as long as we did. How is it possible for a handful of men to hold up a prison for twenty-five days?

I'll always believe the government let the protest go on as long as it did to take the heat off the poll tax riots at Trafalgar Square in London. They started the day before the prison protest and the news soon went global. Our protest was an embarrassment for the government because their prison system was being exposed worldwide, but they still let it carry on.

Every day was a news day, something was always going on. It was a very hot month considering it should have been April showers, but those showers soon came from the Green Goddess fire engines. The water cannons tried to hose some of the lads off the roof, but they found it funny, stripped off and had a nice cold shower – just what they needed after a hot sunny day; I also stripped off one day and waited with a bar of soap while standing on a parapet. Some days it did get a bit dangerous when the water cannons were fired at the lads on the very top of the roof; they could easily have been swept off by the force of the water while the screws looked on, laughing and taunting.

I remember my last day on the roof very clearly. I was sunbathing, it was a very hot day; it had gone very quiet down below. Then my friend John Murray (John-John) came over and said one of the screws wanted to speak to me. I was the main negotiator and they wanted me to go down to talk.

So I walked towards E-wing via the hospital gates. There were two screws, a male officer named Tate and a female officer named Jones. While we were exchanging conversation, Tate's body language didn't seem right. He was twitching and fidgeting.

I backed away and got ready to make a run for it as I had a feeling it was a set-up. As I turned round the cell doors behind me opened and out came the riot squad. There were far too many to count. They came running out and blocked my way. I knew then it was over for me.

Although I ran at them it was inevitable that I was going to end up captured and restrained. Still, I wasn't going to give up easily. I hoped we'd done enough to bring justice to those who brought injustice to the prisoners.

I was taken to a cell on the hospital wing and, about an hour later, put into a white boiler suit to have my photo taken like a prized trophy. One of the screws even pulled my head back so people could take a good look at their catch. I was then taken via a waiting van to Astley Bridge Police Station in Bolton, Greater Manchester. I wasn't given any physical abuse by the screws or riot squad when I was captured, as they knew they were now under the watchful eyes of the world media. It would have been a further embarrassment to take the usual liberties.

CHAPTER THIRTEEN

ESCAPE FROM ASTLEY BRIDGE

I was in Astley Bridge Police Station from 23 April 1990, until my escape on 12 June. I was placed in a woman's police cell opposite the sergeant's desk, segregated from the other cells so that they could keep a watchful eye on me.

I was on a hunger strike to support the lads who were still on the roof at Strangeways, but it only lasted two more days because they decided to end the protest on the twenty-fifth day, on account of my capture. I was checked over less and less in the police station as time went on, even though they had adequate security. I could see they were lackadaisical in some aspects of their security measures, especially while the World Cup was on and they were watching the football instead of manning the station.

Then I had a visit from my mate Billy Gould, who wanted

to make sure I was alright. All sorts of rumours were flying around but it wasn't that bad at Astley Bridge. I was left alone; I was able to take a shower every morning; the shower was round the corner from my cell; there were two sets of keys in the container that opened various doors, mainly cell doors and gates.

I couldn't believe it when I was taken for my shower and, when I got back to my cell, a set of keys had been left on the window ledge. I immediately thought it was a set-up but didn't disclose the whereabouts of the keys to anyone. As soon as my cell door was locked I hid the keys in my toilet, inside the flush system. I couldn't sleep well that night because my adrenalin was rushing. One side of me wanted to get out that night but something was telling me to wait, as I truly believed it was a set-up.

I kept the keys for five weeks. I thought it was not just a coincidence that a bunch of keys were left in my cell. I truly believed I was being set up so they could get rid of me because of what happened at Strangeways. I was a high-profile prisoner and an embarrassment to the regime. At that point I was also a suspect in the death of a sex offender during the riots.

Somehow I just know that if I'd escaped that night I probably wouldn't be here now and you wouldn't be reading this book. I'd been warned in the past by a close friend who overheard a police officer talking about having me 'wasted' (done in and got rid of), so I know it was on the cards for me at some point.

I waited until it felt right to go. I tried various keys

when the hatch was down while the officers were watching the football, until I found out which key belonged to my door. Every time I went out of the cell I'd try various doors without the police noticing, until I'd found my route out of there. It didn't take long before I found out which key fitted each lock.

In the end I decided to go in the early hours of one Sunday morning. They used to check me every ninety minutes, so I had to make sure I left all my belongings in my cell. I made my sleeping bag up to look like I was still asleep inside it.

Next I left quietly and made my way out towards the visiting room near the front of the police station. Unfortunately, the key that I thought would fit the main door wasn't the right one. There were only cell-door keys on the bunch I had.

I could not believe it; my heart was beating like a drum. I thought, *this is it*. I'd come this far and now I was stuck.

So I hid in the closed visitors' area for a while. I could see the sergeant's desk from an angle and hid behind the door, thinking of my next move. I knew time was running out and someone would soon be going on their rounds.

The next minute I heard a female police officer ask to be buzzed in. I stood in the passageway and managed to catch the door when she walked through, just before it clicked closed behind her. I was very close to her, but I had to take that chance. I couldn't believe my luck when I got through unnoticed, but all she needed to do was turn round and it was game over.

Then I was stuck in the lobby area, between the back door

leading into the police station and the door that would lead to my freedom. But which door that was I just didn't know.

I looked through the back door and could see what looked like a tearoom for the police officers. To my right there was a generator room, so I knew I couldn't get out there. To my left there was another door, I assumed to the front of the police station. It had a metal plate that I thought could have been an electronic device to open the door automatically. But when I put my hand on it nothing happened.

What the hell am I going to do?

I felt sick because I'd waited so long for this chance and it was all going wrong. But I was determined to get out of there somehow.

So I waited a while, thinking of my next step. Then I heard footsteps coming towards the door. I made a dash for the generator room just in time. I hid behind the door, but in a split second left on tiptoes going after the female officer.

I knew there was a slight delay before the door closed completely. I waited for her to go through then, still on my tiptoes and trying to be as quiet as possible, I managed to get through to the other side.

Now I was in the lobby and had to move fast. All it needed was for the officer to turn round, or even see my shadow, and that was the end of the road for me.

I got through without her seeing me and pushed open the door to the tearoom as quietly as I could. It was all clear. I went over to the fridge to see if there was anything I could drink before I got out, or got caught. I drank some milk and tried to figure a way to get out of there.

Next I tried a key in the back door that led out to the car park. It opened the door. I was almost out and free.

I needed to get away from the police station as soon as possible, but just before I left I noticed a sign in/out book. It did cross my mind to write, 'Lord signing out – have a nice day,' but it may have given my escape away earlier than I anticipated.

Luckily I had a head start with the bogus Alan Lord stuffed inside my cell. I'd have loved to see their faces when they came to wake me up, especially as the screws from Wakefield were en route to escort me to their prison.

I exited the police station from the back, walking down the side of the car park and out into the road. I couldn't believe how easy it was to get through the police station with a bunch of keys in my hand, although I had a close call when a police van came down the road and drove up the driveway I'd just walked down. Lucky escape!

Then I ran over to the fields in front of the station and threw the keys away one by one. I was feeling sheer joy at escaping and the adrenalin was kicking in, giving me the strength to run. I could feel the fresh air on my face and the smell of the trees. I felt fantastic. I remember looking up at the sky and shouting, 'Freedom, freedom at last!'

For a while I was running and then slowed to walking. But it felt like I was walking round in circles, I just didn't know where I was or where I was going. I walked down the field towards the town centre, where I could see bright lights in the distance. I was looking for a road sign that would lead me towards Liverpool, as it was where my friend Vince lived.

I'd spent some time in prison with Vince and he said if I was ever in any kind of trouble to go to his house. (I always kept his address in a safe place – my head!)

I came to a wall at the end of the field and climbed over it, ending up in a graveyard. I decided to walk through; walking amongst the dead didn't unnerve me in the slightest, even though it was dark and I had no way of knowing where I was going. I was just focused on getting as far away from Bolton as possible.

Having reached the other side of the graveyard and climbed over another wall, I walked down the embankment, and ended up slipping into a stream. I was soaking wet but had to keep moving. I walked back up the embankment until I came across some railway tracks. I decided to stay on the tracks instead of going towards the town centre. I started jogging on the sleepers because I knew I was safe and out of sight. I also knew the tracks would eventually lead somewhere instead of my going round and round in circles.

Deciding to follow left, I was jogging for what seemed to be hours but slowed down as the land opened up. I could see open land for miles and it'd been years since I'd witnessed such a scene of beauty. It was light by this time but I still had no idea where I was heading. I walked for a while until I could see a built-up area in the distance. I could smell the sea in the air as I headed towards a coastal town. After another half-hour of walking I was in Southport.

I got off the tracks and walked down towards the town, to the seafront, and sat for a while looking out towards the sea.

I walked across the road to a penny arcade to get a drink of water and use the toilet for a wash-down.

When I came out I asked a parking attendant for directions to the railway station, which wasn't that far away. I went to the ticket office and told the clerk my car had been stolen with all my belongings, and I had no way of getting home. The clerk, who was a scouser, let me have a free ticket to Bootle, near Liverpool. I hadn't been on a train for years; everything seemed new to me and I just stared out of the window all the way to Merseyside.

And when I finally got there I felt a sense of relief. I knew that once I got to my mate Vince's house I'd be looked after and would get some food. I was desperate for a place to stay and get my head down.

I got a taxi and told the driver to take me to Vince's address; I knew it'd be safe there as it wasn't on my prison records. When I arrived at his house I was going to do a runner from the taxi a few yards down the road, as I had no money. But when the taxi was on Vince's street I noticed someone coming out of his house. I told the driver to pull up outside his house and that I'd only be a minute.

I asked the guy coming out of Vince's house to pay the taxi for me and went to the front door, hoping he'd think I was a relative. He paid and came back to let me in, because there was no one in the house. I told him I was a friend of Vince's and needed to speak to his wife, so he got on his mobile to her.

Vince's wife soon came back with her friend and told me Vince was still in prison and not due to be released for a couple of weeks. I couldn't believe it, but she said she'd sort something out for me. She was very nice and hospitable; she made me something to eat, let me use her bathroom and even gave me some clothes to get changed into.

While I was in the bath I heard the front door and voices downstairs. For a minute I didn't know if I'd been recognised in Merseyside. But Vince's wife shouted for me to come down quickly and leave fast with the boys who'd come to take me to a safe house. All I had was a towel wrapped round my waist; the lads told me they'd go out as soon as I got to the safe house to buy me some clothes and shoes.

I stayed there for four days. I was just chilling and eating good food that I hadn't tasted for such a long time. I read the papers about my escape and the so-called dangerous man who should not be approached. It was a load of rubbish, just scaremongering tactics. They used to make me out to be a monster because I was an embarrassment to the police authorities. I was being hunted like a mass murderer or nutcase because they could not uphold their so-called high security in their state-of-the-art police station, which was supposed to have the best security system in Greater Manchester. I must have pissed quite a few pigs off that day.

While staying at the safe house there was a plan put in place to get me out of the country. I'd had an offer of help from a woman who worked to resettle prisoners and was interested in my cause. She was very interested when she found out about me being in Astley Bridge Police Station and labelled as the ringleader. She told me she'd noticed me when she was on a visit with an offender's mother, and that she wanted to help.

After only her first visit I could tell from her body language and flirting manner that she liked me in more than a professional way. But I wasn't interested in her like that, she wasn't my type. I just thought she might be able to help me so I was being friendly towards her. She kept in touch with me while I was at Astley Bridge.

I met the woman again when one of the lads brought her down to the safe house to help me get out of the country. The lads went to meet her to make sure she wasn't being followed. They even made a detour and used three cars to check her out – one to bring her to the safe house and two to check she wasn't being followed. I just had to force myself to believe she was genuinely going to help me. She said she could take me over to Ireland and help me get out of the country at a later date.

The plan was for me to go straight away but I wanted to stay on in Merseyside for a few days. It was a stupid mistake.

Looking back now, I think I was set up by the woman. Something didn't add up about her. I also think she knew, after spending a few hours with me in the safe house, that I wasn't interested in her in any way other than as help to get me out of the country.

On the fourth night of my escape I was waiting to be taken down to the shipping dock. She'd arranged for me to go with her to the docks at midnight to board a boat. With hindsight, I don't think anyone was even at the docks to take me to

Ireland. How would they get across the Mersey at that time of night without being noticed?

While I was sat waiting to go down to the docks, I heard a helicopter above the house hovering in circles. I'd already told the lads, 'If it comes on top I'm straight out of the window.' So off I went: bang out of the back window, through the garden.

The garden was full of police officers and the riot squad, one of whom came at me with a pickaxe but missed. I jumped to my left and could see at least thirty police surrounding me. I jumped up on the wall, and one of them said, 'Come on, Lord, give yourself up!' I told him to fuck off and called them a load of bastards.

I could see people looking through the window next door, so I jumped down into their garden, smashed their back window in and jumped through it. I then ran through the house and smashed through the front window. I just kept going through the windows of about six different houses to escape.

When I smashed through one window, I landed on top of the television and rolled off it, knocking it to the floor. There was a man still sat in his chair and a woman screaming at me. I said 'sorry' but had to keep running to the back room, smashing in the back-door window to get out.

And when I went through the last house I hid in the coal bunker in the backyard, placing some wood over its opening to camouflage myself. The helicopter seemed to have disappeared, but I knew there was still an army of police out there.

It was a plainclothes officer who found me hiding in the bunker. He was in the backyard looking around with a torch. He called for backup and they all surrounded me.

They dragged me out, threw me to the floor, handcuffed me, lifted me up in the air and took me back through the last house I'd run through and out the front door. They then threw me into a waiting van.

I was taken to a Liverpool police station – after receiving a good hiding, of course. I stayed there overnight before they took me on to Wakefield prison. I was gutted that I was caught after only five days; I just wish I'd left the safe house earlier.

And I was only in Wakefield for a few days too; it was there that I met Tony Erdmann, who'd become a very close friend. But I was eventually taken back to Frankland dispersal prison.

CHAPTER FOURTEEN

SUNDAY MORNING BLUES

When I got to Frankland prison, I was told to put an escapee's prison uniform on. I refused. I told the screw I was already a Category-A prisoner and had to walk around with a guard and his blue security book, marking down my every move. There was no way I was going around with stripes all over me as well.

I only remained in Frankland Prison for twenty-eight days because it kicked off big-style on my wing. I was on D-wing when it started. The screws decided that things were going to change on Sundays; we were all going to be locked up in the mornings while they did some training in the gym. It was a load of rubbish; they just wanted to lock us up so they could read their papers and drink tea without any interaction or disturbance from the inmates.

We were all pissed off and made a collective decision to barricade the landing if they locked us up for their convenience. It was going round the landing that we would barricade D-wing the following Sunday, but the funny thing is that the inmates who were giving it the big 'un and mouthing off about what they were going to do ended up staying in their cells and turning a blind eye. It was the quieter ones who got on with it.

Nothing was sorted out and the screws said they were going to lock us up on the following Sunday. So when Sunday came around we started barricading the landing, bringing as much furniture as possible. A few of the lads were getting verbal with the screws on the other side and insisting that negotiations had to take place. As the landing was barricaded up, we had to talk through the window at the end.

They knew at the end of the day that we were going to stand our ground, but they chose to ignore our request to sort the problem out. So we stayed there all night, taking it in turns to sleep for an hour or two; there were about forty-five of us protesting.

It wasn't long before we heard a commotion at the end of the landing and the riot squad arriving. They started cutting the gates down where we'd barricaded ourselves in with furniture. But while they were using the cutters the furniture caught fire and smoke poured down the landing. I noticed some burning furniture had fallen near the door of an inmate named Mickey.

I went over to Mickey's cell and asked if he wanted me to get him out. He said he was alright, even though he was the

114

first to open his mouth about the barricade and the first to lock up when it all kicked off. I found out years later he was a rapist – no wonder he ran to his cell and hid in the corner when we started moving the furniture.

The lads and I were on the other side of the wing that faced the Astro Turf pitch, so we could see fire engines and dog handlers coming in. The dog handlers were laughing and mocking us cynically. 'Keep on laughing, you bastards,' I told one of them, 'we're coming for you to knock that smile off your fucking face!'

We went over to 'the quiet room' (which wasn't that quiet most of the time), took a door off its hinges and carried it to the window to smash through it. We couldn't believe it when, after only a few hits, the whole frame came out including the surrounding bricks. The first person out was my mate John from Ardwick Green in Manchester; I jumped out after him and then the dog handler who was laughing at us came towards me.

I told him to keep the dog away, but he was taunting me and set it on me. I picked up a stick to keep it away, but the dog jumped up at me and started biting my arm. I had to whack it on the head to protect myself. The dog ran behind him but the screw pulled it back towards me, commanding it to attack me. The dog was barking mad and looked like it was going for me again.

Of course I had to defend myself. Even though I didn't want to harm the dog, I had no choice but to hit it again to stop it getting at my arm and legs. This time the dog collapsed and fell down on the floor.

115

Then the riot squad came round the corner with their shields. There were only four of us and I knew we didn't stand a chance, so two of the lads ran in the opposite direction and my mate Owen and I ran to the window we'd climbed out of. I told Owen to jump up first and I'd give him a leg-up, but he shouted for me to hurry up so I started climbing and told him I'd pull him up once I was back in. But before I could get a tight grip of him, he was dragged back down by the riot squad. They jumped on him.

They put their riot shields up against the window so I couldn't see what they were doing to Owen. But I could hear them laying into him. He was badly cut and ended up with deep scars.

Some of the lads decided collectively that negotiations were over and enough was enough. It was over but I decided I'd go out last. The lads went out one by one, but the first one out got dragged to the recess area and his face smashed into the sink, causing serious damage.

The governor and other screws intervened because they'd never seen that level of violence. But I'd been around the system long enough to know full well the brutality that went on behind certain prison walls. Having to put up with derogatory remarks on a daily basis until I was provoked into altercations with the screws, it was always me against numbers, never one-to-one. If it wasn't the screws coming in my cell to kick the shit out of me, it was the control and restraint team bouncing all over me. There were so many occasions when I was beaten up badly that it's hard for me to remember the worst beating I have ever had. Many times

I thought they'd gone too far and I'd never recover from my injuries, but I always bounced back. The screws knew they could lay into me at any time and leave me in my cell for days on end until I recovered.

I just wished it was me they'd caught instead of Owen, because I was due back in court for the Strangeways trial and I'd have loved to see their faces if I'd turned up with my face smashed in. They'd have seen at first hand what we prisoners had to put up with.

While I was getting ready to leave, I saw this Asian lad with a music system in his hands. He'd taken it from the cell of a prisoner named Jerry, from Chicago. I asked the lad what he was doing with the music system; he said he was looking after it.

'No you're not, you're trying to fucking rob it!'

So I told him to put it back in Jerry's cell and get out. He put it back without saying a word.

I went out shortly after him, checking there was no one else left inside. I climbed over, jumped down and was immediately surrounded by the riot squad.

The first C&R officer I saw was an old PE instructor called Brian Nicholson. I'd bumped into him before in Wakefield Prison, we'd exchanged a few verbals in the gym.

'Oh, we meet again, do we?' I said.

He sort of smirked and said, 'Come on, Lord, move along.'

Then two screws handcuffed me and put me in the Cat-A van waiting to take me and one of the IRA guys. When we got into the van there were another five lads in there. They took us all to Hull Prison.

CHAPTER FIFTEEN

HUNGER WITH A VIEW

When we got to Hull, I was put straight in the segregation unit. I'd escaped a good hiding this time, for some reason; I guess they'd already taken it out on the other lads they caught first.

While I was in Hull Prison I had a room with a view; I was able to see the River Humber. I remember one night looking through the window; I could see a boat all lit up, it looked amazing. I shouted out of my window to the other lads so they could see it. We were all on hunger strike and into our seventh day. I was starting to feel a little bit weak because I was still keeping up my fitness training.

After eight days of being there, I was called down to see my solicitor, Mary Monson, and my barrister, Keith Harrison, on the segregation unit. Keith told me I had to eat something because I needed some strength for the trial and to take notes. But I refused.

'No, I cannot do it – I have to stay on the hunger strike with the lads.'

I must have looked a mess. We talked for a while but nothing was registering with me. They were preparing notes but must have realised I wasn't paying much attention.

Mary found out who else was on the hunger strike and called one of the Irish lads down to see her. She asked him if it was alright for me to come off so I could prepare for the Strangeways Prison trial, but before he could answer her I shouted, 'No, I am sticking to the hunger strike, I am with the lads!'

She just ignored me and asked him if he and the other lads smoked.

'We all do, Miss.'

Mary asked him if they had any cigarettes.

'No, Miss.'

I knew what was coming next.

'If I supply you and the lads with tobacco, will you exclude Alan from the hunger strike?'

I shouted, 'No!' But she just ignored me.

The Irish lad said to Mary that he'd speak to the others and come back to her shortly. It wasn't long before he told Mary and me that they'd reached an agreement and we'd all come off the hunger strike together. I was so pissed off with her because she'd got her own way, but even though I wasn't happy about the situation I didn't want the lads to miss out on their tobacco. So I agreed to come off the strike with them.

While the visit was continuing, one of the officers came to the door and told me I was being moved straight out. I was surprised and so was Mary.

I didn't have much time to say my goodbyes. I just got my things together and told one of the lads I'd phone and let him know where I was being moved to. I was glad to see the back of Hull seg unit, especially as they'd tried to stitch me up as soon as I got there: I was put on adjudication and placed on a disciplinary report, on a charge of killing a prison officer. I couldn't believe what I was hearing.

'I don't know what you're talking about,' I told the adjudication hearing. 'I've *never* killed a prison officer.'

'You are charged with killing a serving dog,' the officer in charge said, 'and killing a serving dog is the same as killing a prison officer.'

I thought this must be some kind of joke. Then I remembered the case of a man called Oberdine from Africa, a big merchant seaman who went to stay in a lodging house somewhere in Wales. He was used to cooking in a certain way which the landlord wasn't happy about, and an argument broke out between them. The police were called and a dog handler set his charge on Oberdine; the dog ended up dead because Oberdine hit it in the face while defending himself. He was charged with killing the dog and sentenced to fourteen years in prison.

Then I started to panic. I was already facing another ten years added onto my sentence for the Strangeways Prison riots. I did a lot of thinking and stood my ground, telling the disciplinary board I wasn't going to be punished for defending myself from an attack by a vicious dog.

'If you are going to charge me with killing the dog you have to follow the right procedure and bring in the RSPCA.'

Next the dog handler came in to give evidence. It was all a bit pathetic. I was already in dispersal prison, in the segregation unit and serving a life sentence, so there wasn't much more they could do to me. They knew I was going to take them to the European Court of Human Rights and kick up a fuss so the charge was dropped. Hypothetically, if someone killed a police dog while protecting themselves they wouldn't be charged with killing a police officer, so why would this be the case with a prison dog? It didn't make sense.

I was taken to Parkhurst Prison but I was only there for just under two weeks. We called the prison 'Cooper's Troopers' because the prisoners on F-wing had psychological problems and their psychiatrist was Dr Cooper. It was just like *One Flew over the Cuckoo's Nest*. I got another visit from Mary Monson, who stayed down an extra day because Keith Harrison was also coming down the next day; they told me they'd try to get me moved back up north because it was ridiculous being in the Isle of Wight while the Strangeways trial was going on in Manchester. But the Home Office claimed I was better off anywhere other than in a northern prison because of confrontation with the screws. Mary told me she'd see what she could do to have me moved out as soon as possible.

There were sometimes rumours going around the southern prisons that I was some kind of a hard-man, not to be approached and very dangerous, but that came from the screws making me out to be a madman. At Parkhurst one of the lads who knew me from the North came down to see me; Perry told me someone from the landing upstairs was telling people I was a sex offender who served time in Strangeways, but it was soon put right when they found out who I was.

Another lad came to tell me that he was going to do in whoever was slagging me off, but I said to leave it. I was well known throughout the prison system and gained respect for fighting against the regime. There were inmates that I'd met from the dispersal system in Parkhurst, but I'd deal with this myself.

I went up to see him in his cell but I could see someone had already got to him. He was frightened and shaking, with his head down to the floor, I just told him to get his fucking facts straight before he started spreading rumours about me, or he'd have to face me next time.

CHAPTER SIXTEEN

THE STRANGEWAYS TRIAL

When I came back to my cell from the gym to get my toiletries, there was a screw at my door who told me I was being moved out. I had a shower and went to the reception area. When I got there some northern screws were waiting for me.

'Where do you think you're going dressed like that, Lord?' one of them said to me. 'You can't travel like that, in them clothes.'

'Why not, what's your problem?' I was wearing a tracksuit.

There was already tension brewing between myself and the northern screws, so one of the reception screws called for security. The security screws came to the reception area and told the northern screws I could go in the clothes I had on if I wanted to.

'This is our prison and he travels how we say, not you.'

I laughed because I knew how the southern screws didn't like the northern screws, and vice versa.

Then I was put in the van and taken to Full Sutton, just outside York. It was more convenient for my legal team because it was much closer to Manchester. I was there about eighteen months and it wasn't that bad. I still had the same routine wherever I ended up: I stripped my cell down to the bare necessities, bleached my cell out and placed my clothes and toiletries in there with just a sheet on the floor.

I got my head down and carried on preparing my legal paperwork for the Strangeways trial. I kept myself busy and out of trouble. Then, one day while I was on the phone to my brief, an old acquaintance from Newcastle called Nigel told me it was all kicking off. My brief could hear what Nigel was saying and advised me not to get involved. But I told him, 'If the lads need my help I'll be there for 'em,' and hung up.

Nigel told me Owen Hepburn had been beaten up badly again. He had been wrapped up and taken to the seg unit, apparently over Owen's vegan dietary requirements. He had been refused what he needed and started raising his voice, storming off back to his cell. Later, he was thrown around in his cell.

So I went to see what was going on. The lads were stood around talking about what happened to Owen; they were all fuming and made a collective decision to kick-off when the screws let them out for association. I didn't know anything about what had happened or what was being planned until

Nigel told me. One of the lads said the others wanted me to go outside with them, as I was renowned as a good negotiator and high-profile prisoner.

I couldn't let them or Owen down and agreed to go with them, to find out what the screws had to say. By the time I got there I could see one of the lads had a bunch of keys in his fist and a couple of screws had been punched and kicked around. To my right, the governor, Rowett, was pinned against the wall with blades held against his stomach.

One of the lads shouted, 'If you don't send some of the screws to release Owen and bring him back to us from the unit, you and the prison are going down!'

I intervened, telling the governor to take me and my mate, a lifer called Scottish John, down to the block to see Owen and check he was alright. He agreed. We went down and waited in the visitors' area. The governor came back with his second-in-command and Owen – but Owen came to meet us on crutches.

The lads were right. Owen told us one of the screws had poured boiling hot water down his leg. John screamed at the governor and threatened to smash him all over the place. I was a bit more diplomatic as I knew they were already in a lot of trouble for what they'd done to Owen. By doing things the right way he'd get compensation. I calmed John down and told him now was not the time. They agreed to let Owen back up on the wing where the lads could look after him.

I told the governor: 'Just because you've let Owen up, don't think you can start shipping people out who are witnesses to his assault over the next couple of days, because it'll all kick-off again.'

He knew there would be consequences if he did, but I knew full well what was going to happen. I'd seen it all before.

Owen came back up on his crutches. We got a solicitor to take photos of his legs and put a complaint in. It was only a matter of a few weeks before some of the lads involved in the disturbance were secretly shipped out. Surprisingly, I remained at Full Sutton because my brief would not have me moved anywhere else.

The Strangeways Prison trial soon came round. I stayed at central detention in Manchester during the week and was taken back to Full Sutton at the weekend. I was charged with murdering Derek White, the sex offender who died during the protest. I was also charged with being the ringleader, alongside Paul Taylor, of Britain's worst prison riots.

I did not kill White. It'd been proven that he died of a blood clot and I wasn't involved. I'd be acquitted alongside four other inmates; neither was I the ringleader of the Strangeways Prison riots. It had always been a collective decision to demonstrate for our human rights against the brutality of the prison regime.

During the trial I was escorted by the screws from Full Sutton, who handed me over to the police at central detention centre in Manchester from Monday to Friday. One day, while I was in the dock, the judge, Lord Chief Justice Woolf, called a recess because the microphone was broken. I was the last one left in the dock and was talking to Sarda, the legal clerk from my solicitor's firm, through the glass.

'You, get downstairs now!' the screw to the side of me shouted.

'Are you talking to me?' I asked him.

'Yes, now get down those stairs!' he shouted back.

'Well, when you talk to me in a respectful manner in front of private citizens, that is when I'll answer you. But until then you can go away.'

'Alan, can you go downstairs please?' pleaded the screw on the other side of me.

'That's better,' I said. But my mind was already made up as to what I was going to do.

I stood up and walked towards the back of the dock. Before I went down the stairs, I said to the screw who spoke to me like a piece of shit, 'You've got a bit of a dogmatic manner, you, haven't you?'

'So what?'

He stood glaring at me with a clipboard in his hand. I slapped him hard right in the face; he went straight back into the glass, threw his clipboard down and ran at me. He tried to punch me but I stepped to the side and he missed. I punched him again and this time he went flying over the chairs, landing in the dock.

The other screw tried to grab hold of me but I shook him off and threw him to one side. He ran down the stairs. Then my verbal abuser came at me again, but I picked him up, threw him down the stairs and ran after him. He jumped up but I grabbed hold of him and gave him a good hiding. I told him never to speak to me like that again.

Then I was restrained by police officers who climbed into

the dock after me. I told them I didn't have a problem with them, and that it was the screws from Full Sutton who had an attitude problem with me.

I was taken back to the holding cell but nothing more came of it. When the lads found out what had gone on they wanted to kick-off with the screws, but I told them to leave it because it wouldn't go down well with the jury.

We were all called back upstairs after the recess. I couldn't believe it when the same screw was still smirking at me. I got so mad that I pinned him against the glass.

'Do you want to continue where we left off, dickhead? You have your boys, but this time I have mine. So what will it be, eh?'

'I don't want any trouble,' he said and put his head down. So I backed off and it was left at that. The trial continued without any further hiccups.

We went back to Full Sutton. Nothing else was mentioned on the way back, but on Saturday morning my door was unlocked and a senior screw off my wing said he was placing me on adjudication for assaulting a prison officer.

'What prison officer?'

He said I had to go down to the segregation unit with him in front of a female governor, who was horrible. She asked me how I was pleading on the charge put before me.

I told them I was not under the supervision of the prison service at the time of the incident, but under crown court proceedings and they had no right to put me on report. I told the governor that, if they wanted to charge me with assault, I'd have to get witnesses.

'What witnesses would those be, Mr Lord?'

'All the barristers, solicitors, and other witnesses that were in the court on that day, and you'd have to take into consideration that some of my witnesses might not be able to make the hearing at your beck and call. It could also take months before they could put the evidence together, but it's not a problem for me because I have all the time in the world. I'm not going anywhere. So provided no one decides to leave a set of keys laying around for me, I'll be on my way.'

She looked at me with a raised eyebrow. She said she'd let me know in due course what was going to happen. I went back to my cell and didn't hear anything else about it. I knew they wouldn't take it any further because it'd only expose the way they conducted things in their prison. They didn't want *that* to happen.

The trial carried on for around three months. Eventually the murder and riot charges got thrown out because it was found out that Derek White had actually died of a pulmonary embolism, or blood clot, that travelled from behind his left knee. He was prone to heart attacks, as they found out during the course of the trial.

White had been on remand for child sex-abuse charges and placed on the sex offenders' wing. When it all kicked-off, I heard that some of the lads had got scaffolding poles, and that White and some other paedophiles had been attacked and beaten, but none were killed.

I was nowhere near the sex offenders' wing; I was on the roof and had nothing to do with any attacks on anyone. White had a blood clot that could have dislodged at any given time, as the coroner admitted. Jeffrey Garrett, the pathologist, admitted he'd made a mistake with his diagnosis; he originally said injuries sustained in Strangeways Prison had caused the death of Derek White, but after an independent pathologist was brought in by the defendants' QCs, Garrett also said he had mixed up the tissue vials while performing the autopsy.

The jury was sent out by the judge on technicalities. He then said to the prosecution that, as a result of the findings, the case was dismissed. There were nine of us stood in the dock, including Paul Taylor, John Spencer and other lads I'd never seen before. It was a great relief because I thought I was going to be stitched up for good. It just goes to show how easily manipulated the justice system can be. I felt like I was being set up for murdering Derek White because they wanted to make an example of me for my defiance. They wanted me out of the way and if I'd been convicted of a second murder I'd never get out; the key would have been thrown away.

While I was being interviewed at Astley Bridge Police Station before the trial, a police officer told me seven witnesses had come forward who said they'd seen me attack Derek White and throw him over the balcony. I asked him what inducements they'd been given. He just smirked at me and looked smug. But they had not one piece of CCTV footage showing me destroying property or even throwing a stone. I was on that roof protesting for prisoners' rights in Strangeways Prison and that was that.

When the jury eventually came back into the court, I was cleared of the murder and riot charges. The charges were dismissed by Lord Chief Justice Woolf, who clearly emphasised to the prosecution that 'further charges are not to be proceeded with against any of these men'.

This is where stupidity comes into play. Michael Mansfield, one of the best QCs in the country, told Taylor and Spencer not to give evidence and they'd walk away from the riot charge, just as I was advised. But they went ahead, smirking and telling the jury about how the sex offenders deserved what they got. When the sex offenders were giving evidence, Taylor and Spencer were pulling faces and intimidating them. When the jury went out to consider their verdict, it wasn't long before they came back in and found them guilty. The judge sentenced them both to a further ten years in prison. I couldn't believe it. All they'd needed to do was keep their big mouths shut and follow the instructions of Mansfield.

While the trial was going on, four out of the seven inmates that had made statements against me had retracted them. None of them even knew me personally. One had to be subpoenaed because he changed his mind and didn't want to go ahead with his statement. The other two stuck to theirs, which I thought was obviously in the hope of an early release, but they need never have given a statement against me because I was never charged with the murder of Derek White.

During the prosecution's opening speech he said, and I quote: 'Anyone who stayed in the prison (that being inside the prison or on the roof), after the first day of April 1990, deliberately stayed to commit riot and therefore is guilty of riot,' unquote. A Queen's Counsel called Jameson clearly demonstrated the absurdity of that statement by pointing out that over 300 prisoners were protesting on the roof after the first day of April 1990, yet few were charged. He went on to say that the charges were made up and the prisoners handpicked as scapegoats.

The Lord Chief Justice said to the prosecution, at the end of the first trial after delivering his verdict, not to proceed against any of the men on the next indictment. But, against Judge Woolf's wishes, I was called alongside nine other men on a six-to-two committal and charged with conspiracy to cause GBH and conspiracy to riot.

I asked the presiding Judge Sack how I could be acquitted from a charge of riot but charged with conspiracy to riot. Either I'd done the act or I hadn't. But they didn't want me to leave the courtroom without some kind of conviction, and conspiracy is the oldest trick in the court's book. I just knew I was being set up and that I needed to get away. I'd be given a further ten years in prison in my absence, as I'd escaped from the courts between the first and second trial – which should never have taken place.

Out of fifty-six men, only twenty-four were charged in the first and second trials. Like Mr Jameson said, they'd already handpicked who they wanted. To my recollection there were at least 300 men on the roof over the first few days and 1,664 prisoners inside the prison after the first day of April 1990. Believe me, they were not all sat down picking their noses. It was always a collective decision to protest and it was made by many men. My sentence was a response to what the Prison Officers Association said in a newspaper article, stating that those responsible should get at least ten years.

I've always told officials and anyone else interested in the truth that I was innocent of the Strangeways Prison riots, just as I've always had my doubts as to whether I should have gone down for murder or manslaughter on the original Gilbert charge. During the second trial the prosecution tried to use my living conditions against me. Once again I quote:

'Is it true that you wake up in the early hours of the morning for circuit training? And is it also true that you live a Spartan life (living without a television, radio, bed frame and furniture)? Would you agree that you are very disciplined? And that someone who is very disciplined, such as yourself, may make a leader? And that you led this incident?'

I naturally refuted the despicable (and bordering on desperate) inferences. Because if my so-called discipline had been viewed from the other end of the spectrum, I've no doubt the prosecution would have vigorously depicted me as someone bored, unmotivated and lacking tenacity, therefore looking for attention in a narcissistic way.

So I told the prosecution I was involved in a justifiable protest against human rights abuses. I didn't cause injury to anyone. I was not responsible for starting fires or damaging prison property. I was there to get across to the public and press the disgraceful treatment that the prisoners had to endure.

The riots were allowed to continue to take the attention off the poll-tax protest that turned into riots in Trafalgar Square, London. The poll-tax riots were starting to spread nationally. All the attention was put onto Strangeways. If the poll-tax riots hadn't been going on, I can guarantee that the Strangeways Prison riots would have been over in a day or two!

Every day the newspapers were full of coverage of Strangeways, most of which was untrue. One headline said there were '20 Dead'; another screamed of multiple bodies left under rubble in F-wing; they even had body bags lying out on the streets, panicking the public and the families of prisoners.

But the riots were left to continue for twenty-five days, even though the number of protesting inmates was less and less; the lads' demonstrating days had come to an end, or they'd simply had enough and wanted to hand themselves in. No one was forced to do anything they didn't want to do.

But I was always going to stay until the bitter end, because the longer we stayed up on the prison roof, the more we got the attention of the world media. It was what we needed to expose the disgraceful British prison regime.

CHAPTER SEVENTEEN

SECOND ESCAPE

The second time I escaped was pure opportunism. It was an opportunity placed right in front of me while we were on trial at the crown court in Manchester.

Our cell doors were left open in between the hearings because they didn't want us locked up all the time, in case it caused any disturbances. One day, while in the recess area talking to an African inmate called Mark Azzopardi, I came across a way out. While Azzopardi was mopping the floor, he lifted the mop up and it happened to hit the top of the ceiling, which was quite low. The sound that came back was very hollow.

We looked at each other. I took the stick off him, went into a toilet cubicle and hit the ceiling. This time the stick went right the way through. I was trying to work out where the recess would lead to if we made a hole big enough to get through. It was risky but we had to try.

We went into the toilet and locked the door behind us. We started hitting the ceiling and it went through very easily. Azzopardi put his head through the hole once we'd made the hole big enough.

'It's huge up here, Al!' he told me.

He jumped down and I made the hole big enough for him to get up and take a look around. He climbed up and along, shouting down to me that it went all the way to the bottom end of the court. He was up there for a few minutes. When he came down, he said there was a way out through the last courtroom.

The adrenalin was kicking in at the prospect of getting out. Deep down, I knew I was going to be stitched up in the second trial, so I wanted to try to get out of the country. I had nothing to lose.

We covered the hole with some white toilet paper and went back to the cells. We told the lads what we'd found, but, unfortunately, some had to be fall guys and stay behind. If we all went the police would get onto it straight away because there'd be no noise. It was an okay atmosphere in there, quite relaxed sometimes though a bit monotonous. As long as there was some banter and laughter going on, they wouldn't suspect anything. The police just sat in their office during the day and let us get on with it until it was time for us to go back up to the dock for trial.

The court usually finished around 4 pm and then the last hour was spent with the legal team. We decided we'd go straight after we'd finished for the day. There were just five of us who were going to try to get out – Azzopardi, John Murray, Tony Bush, Barry Morton and me. We went down to the recess area and I started hitting at the ceiling in the cubicle, where we'd made the hole.

We all got through and crawled across the ceiling to the end of Court Four. It was great, but at the same time nerve wracking, because I wanted to get out so much.

We all stuck together and waited for the right moment to go back down on the other side. We knew the courts closed at around 4 pm, so we waited for ten minutes and then started pushing down on the ceiling. We managed to make a small hole. I just about popped my head through it. There was no one in the court so we had a chance.

We made the hole big enough for the lads to get down, one by one. I was the last but I pulled a lot more ceiling down with me when I was getting through, because of my weight. It made a noise and we held our breath for a few seconds. But no one heard us.

Then we went through Court Four to the back door through the judge's chambers, and then down a corridor. We had no idea where we were going. All we wanted to do was find a door with 'Way Out' on it. Then a man came out of nowhere.

'Can I help you, gentlemen?' he asked.

'Oh yes please,' my mate John said. 'We're doing some roofing work and have got a bit lost, we just need to find the exit.'

'Oh yes, it's just down to the left, then the exit door is on the right.'

'Thanks, mate.'

Off we all went, with sweat pouring down our backs. We followed his directions to a huge wooden door. It had two large bolts on it, so we unlatched them. When the door opened we couldn't believe it: we stepped out right in front of the main entrance of Manchester Crown Court.

As soon as we got down and went through the court, one of the lads asked someone for some money to use the public phone. He phoned someone to come to the side of the court to meet John, Tony and I. Azzopardi and Barry made their own way out of town. After waiting for quite a while I started to get agitated.

'No one is coming for us,' I said to the lads.

I told them to follow me and started walking down to the canal. I couldn't understand why our lift hadn't turned up, but found out later that they were waiting on the other side of the court.

As we walked I saw some black lads dealing at the side of the canal. I went over to them and asked one if he could sort a taxi out for us. I told him he'd understand one day.

He agreed to help us. We waited at the side of the canal and then a private taxi pulled up. The lad told me it was safe and he'd take us anywhere we wanted. I thanked him and told the driver to take us to Liverpool.

John had arranged for someone to meet us in Liverpool and for the taxi to be paid for as soon as we got there. It was by coincidence that I happened to know the taxi driver, from one of the prisons I'd been in. He asked if everything was okay and wanted to help, but I told him everything had been arranged and looked at John. John nodded back as if to say it's all been sorted.

We went to a safe house and we went downstairs into the cellar where we felt safer. John went out to make further arrangements and the girls who lived there looked after us, making us cups of tea and sandwiches.

Then we waited and waited but John didn't come. I started to get a bit concerned in case he'd been caught. The time was ticking away and it'd got to midnight.

'We have to move,' I said, 'John is *not* coming back.'

We went upstairs and Tony made a call to a girl he knew. She had a friend who ran a hotel who said she'd help us.

So we waited for a while before she came over to pick us up. We'd only got about two miles away before we were stopped by a police patrol car. It felt like we'd been set up; we just had to keep calm. I was in the back seat and pulled my hat over my face as if I was asleep. I'd already told Tony, 'If it comes on top we have to fight our way out.' The driver got out because it was her car and she had her documents in order. One of the police officers came over to Tony's side and asked him where we'd been.

'Partying,' he replied.

The copper looked in the back and shone a torch at me.

'What's wrong with your mate?' he asked.

'Oh he's okay, he's just had too much to drink and he's sleeping it off. We're alright.'

I couldn't believe it when we were told to go on our way; it was a close call.

We got to the new house and stayed there till around seven

in the morning. We had to leave early because I'd contacted my good mate Damien Noonan (RIP), who was coming from Salford to pick me up. I knew Damien from Lower Broughton in Manchester when I was a teenager. He was very good friends with Paul Flannery, who I'd grown up with, and he always asked about how I was doing and paid his respects on many occasions down the years.

I didn't know what had happened to John but we couldn't wait around in Liverpool any longer. I met Damien at the Showcase cinema in Liverpool; he gave me a hug and told me, 'You're a free man.' Tony and I got in his car and made our way back to Manchester.

Damien took me to a safe house in Whalley Range and Tony was taken to another one elsewhere. They had to split us up to be on the safe side while arrangements were made for me to get out of the country. The next day another friend of mine, a Pakistani lad I'd first met inside, came to take me to meet up with the lads in Salford; I felt much better for being there. A couple of old mates told me that the lads had chipped in with a bag of cash – £20,000 to be exact. They also had travel documents for me.

I stayed in the safe house during the day and went out for walks at night. After only a short time, one of the lads told me Tony was getting paranoid and wanted to come and stay with me, so they brought him over. I wasn't happy with the situation but I went along with it. Things were taking time but still looking good.

Then one day I noticed a white car pulled up outside the house with two men in suits; they looked so out of place in that area that I decided to go out the back way and climb over the garden fence to take a closer look. After a couple of minutes they drove off. I waited a while to see what direction they were going in, but just before I went back into the house I saw them coming back.

They parked in the same place without getting out of the car. I went back in and told Tony I wasn't staying there any longer. They had to get us moved quickly because I just knew it was coming on top. It'd only be a matter of minutes before the helicopter was hovering above the house.

A friend came straight away and managed to get us out of the house. He took us somewhere else I didn't really like; it was dirty and smelled like stale food, very unclean and untidy. I didn't want to stay there but at that moment in time we had no choice. I was told not to worry about the conditions as it was only for one night while he made other arrangements. It was a temporary hideout, just so we could get our heads down for the night.

Early the following morning it was arranged for us to go to a safe house in Ashton-under-Lyne. I was told it wouldn't be much longer. I was to leave the country the following Monday, and I felt relieved at the prospect of starting a new life.

Tony and I were moved to another house and we stayed there for just under a week. It was very nice, a large Victorian house. I was able to get out and about because it was somewhere out of the way, a more rural area. I went to a gym in an old mill but still felt a bit paranoid, especially when we heard on the news that Barry Morton had been arrested.

We thought they were coming for us next. I was very anxious to get out of the country. I'd been doing all right until they brought Tony to stay with me, but now he was telling me every five minutes that he could hear someone outside. He was driving me mad.

One evening we went out, just to get out of the house. But one of the girls we met said to me that she thought she knew me from somewhere, that I looked familiar.

'No, I think you're mistaken,' I told her. 'I look like a lot of people; I just have one of those faces. I'm not from round here.'

I knew she'd have seen me in the papers or on the news. She kept on staring at me. I just wanted to get out of there, as far away as possible. I was thinking there might be a reward out for me – like there was when I escaped from Astley Bridge in Bolton – and someone would go to the phone to grass me up.

We went back to the car and I had a word with my friend on the quiet about Tony being paranoid. I told him I thought it'd be better if we were separated. I don't know where he took Tony, but I was relieved to be back on my own. It was all becoming a nightmare, but at least I only had myself to think about if it came on top.

I was taken to another relative's in Ashton-under-Lyne. I didn't feel comfortable in the house with just a woman and her children, but she made me a cup of tea and I sat in silence for a while. Then she started telling me that she thought her house was bugged and she was being watched. I felt even more paranoid. The kids were running round and I didn't want the police to come in while they were there. I left some loose change on the floor and one of the kids asked if he could have some money for sweets. I told him to take it all.

So I sat there for two hours until my friend came back to take me somewhere else. It was dirty and it smelled, but I only had to stay overnight so I tried to keep my spirits up. I couldn't sleep and was thinking negative thoughts because I'd been left alone and didn't know what (or if any) arrangements had been made. I felt very deflated and wondered what the hell was going on. Why was I not out of the country after such a long time? I knew they were helping me the best they could, but I couldn't help thinking it was going to come on top soon.

The next day I was taken to meet up with the lads in Salford. I felt much better being there, and when I met up with my old friends. They said they'd be ready first thing on Monday to get me out of the country. It had all been arranged.

I told the lads I needed to get out of the area and asked if I could be moved to somewhere in the country, just till they could arrange for me to get to the port. They arranged for a driver to take me out to Knutsford, Cheshire, near to Manchester airport. I said my goodbyes because it was clear that if I did get out, I wasn't coming back. I couldn't thank the lads enough for their support.

The driver came to pick me up and we set off. As soon as we drove round the corner, near to McDonalds in Salford, I noticed some cars in a convoy, driving very slowly. I told the driver to pull over and I ran over the road; I was going to wait in a phone box till it was clear but, just as I got near, I saw police vans coming fast up the road. Then, out of nowhere, two police cars were coming towards me. I ran across the grass towards some maisonettes. The police cars drove over the grass to cut me off, but I ran as fast as I could towards some large houses and got away.

I knew they'd soon have the dogs out looking for me and could hear the helicopter en route. I leapt as far as I could onto a doorstep; I couldn't believe that the door was slightly opened. I pushed the door all the way open and stood on a ledge in the hallway, looking out of the window. I could see the police running all over the place. I ran upstairs and didn't know where best to hide. There were different doors: I tried all of them and they were all locked, except one in the corner. To my surprise there was no one inside, so I went in and hid at the side of the wardrobes. They were like bedsits.

The next moment I heard the door open and someone walking upstairs. I stood there with my heart in my mouth. The door to the flat opened and a woman popped her head around the corner.

'Who are you?' she asked me.

'It's okay, don't worry,' I tried to reassure her, 'but the police are after me, they're going to be doing house-to-house enquiries soon.'

She looked shocked but she was a local girl from Salford and I had a feeling she'd be alright.

'If you just go back out and come back in half an hour I'll be gone. If the police are outside, don't let them in will you?'

She said, 'Okay,' but I wasn't sure if she'd help me. I noticed the helicopter had gone and for a moment I thought I was safe. But I could hear something downstairs, it sounded like police radios and people talking.

I opened the door a little bit so I could see who was at the bottom of the hallway. I was right, it was the police. I went back in the room and hid behind the bed, but after a couple of minutes the door opened and I heard a voice say, 'Come on, Lord, give yourself up!'

So I stood up. Two police officers were at the door; one ran out of the room and the other one just stood still with a worried look on his face.

'Well, this is a fair cop isn't it?' I said.

I walked over to him and put my hands out. I was hand-cuffed and taken downstairs. There was a sergeant stood at the bottom of the stairs. I said in front of everyone:

'I would just like to say that the woman who lives here, where I was captured, had nothing to do with me being here. The door was open and I let myself in. I do *not* know her and she has nothing to do with my being here today.'

I know how easy it is for the police to pin things on people and didn't want to get the woman in any kind of trouble. I don't know if she told the police I was there or not, and it doesn't really matter. I was surrounded and didn't have a chance.

Finally, I was led away and taken to Salford Crescent Police Station. It was like a circus outside; I should have had some tickets ready to sell, I'd have made a fortune.

I was at Salford Crescent overnight, with three police

officers sat outside my door. I was gutted at having been so close to getting away. I also felt sick for everyone who'd helped me over the past four weeks.

Next day I was taken back to Full Sutton Prison in York. I thought I'd be straight down to the segregation unit, but instead I was put on normal location. I stayed in Full Sutton for one week. One day I was sat on the floor in my cell, just looking into space, when the door opened.

'Get up, you're going to the seg unit,' the copper told me.

'I am not going anywhere,' I responded. Then I saw the control and restraint team coming towards me.

I'd never seen so many of the riot squad in one place. They were all lined up along each side. I had to be escorted down the landing with the whole place overrun with riot squad. Talk about overkill.

'Get off my fucking arm!' I told one of the members of the control and restraint team.

He let go and I walked all the way from A-wing to the seg unit. As I got down there I noticed more riot squad all lined up.

'Who do you think I am, fucking Superman?' I shouted.

I walked into my cell and the door was locked. I couldn't believe they'd gone to all that trouble just to demonstrate they can all stand up in their riot gear in a nice straight line.

CHAPTER EIGHTEEN

BACK TO SEGREGATION

I was kept in the strip cell for three days. On the third day I was sat on the floor when my cell door opened. I was asked if I wanted a shower; I knew then I was out of there. I stood up and was escorted to the showers.

Then I was led back to the seg unit. As I passed the office I noticed the female governor who was outside my cell on Monday, when I refused to go to the seg unit. She was a Scottish bitch and I couldn't stand her; she stood staring at me through the office window. I knocked on it and said to her, 'Who's having chicken tonight then?' I knew I was going to the SSU (Special Security Unit) but she thought I'd be put straight back into the segregation unit with very little or nothing to eat. The SSU, in contrast, was self-sufficient.

She snarled at me and turned away.

I was given a clean set of clothes, led to the reception area and handcuffed. The head security screw was waiting for me.

'Glad to get rid of you, Lord, good riddance,' he said.

I was taken to the waiting van and then on to Parkhurst Prison. I'd been in there before and didn't mind the governor. She was at reception waiting for me when I checked in.

'What's it like to be back here, Lordy?' she asked.

'It's a relief,' I told her.

She told me I'd be going in the SSU. In fact I was classified as the twenty-third prisoner to be placed within the confines of the SSU. To me it was some kind of joke, because I didn't see myself as a high risk to anyone. I just wanted to get away from incarceration in a barbaric prison system and get out of the country. I wasn't a dangerous person and no one need fear me. Yes, I'd escaped twice, but it was to make a fresh start.

I was put in the special unit with the IRA lads. They were alright with me and we got on. We used to cook together; a guy named Dingus looked after me with food. When I first went down, he took me to the kitchen, opened the pantry door and gave me lots of food and drink.

There was only one of the lads I didn't get on with; he was an idiot and thought he ran the unit, but we soon sorted it out, He was trying it on with me, trying to rule when and where I ate. I let him carry on for a while; then I went to his cell and asked him outright if he wanted to fight me and get it out of the way. But he talked his way out of it, explaining that he thought I was being funny because I wasn't sitting down and eating at the same time as him and the other lads.

'I eat, piss and shit when I want to,' I told him, 'not when someone tells me or expects me to.'

I told him I liked my own space and didn't need to follow his routine. We cleared things up and from that day he was alright with me.

There was only me on one side of the seg unit – which was good, I liked it that way. I had three cells to myself; one had my clay pots in, as I'd started pottery classes to pass the time. They wouldn't let me have a baking kiln for obvious reasons, so the screws had to carry my work over after it'd been in the kiln. It was so funny to watch because they had to carry it across on a wooden board so it wouldn't get damaged. Sometimes I made the smallest, strangest shapes just to watch them struggle bringing the pieces across to me.

The third cell was where I used to keep my gym stuff and my weights. It was a routine that passed away the time fast. I used to train with Jerry, one of the IRA lads, who I got on well with. I wasn't interested in anything political or the tit for tat between England and Ireland. We were all doing our time for the crimes that we'd personally committed and we just had to get on with it.

I enjoyed the outdoors in the summer months at Parkhurst, we used to go out to play tennis. One of the lads had sent me some Timberland boots which I used to play tennis in until I wore the soles out; we used to get the tennis balls, sign our names on them and hit them over the fence, like a message in a bottle. It was always good to get out in the fresh air; it was at times like that when your imprisonment became a little more bearable. But you were soon reminded where you were when it came to lock-up time and the power-happy screws tried to intimidate you.

And I enjoyed the gym in Parkhurst. I'd altered the weights with some tools in the multiple gym, and sawed the circuit bars so we could put more weights on. It was much better for us.

But the physical instructor came in the next day and asked, 'What's happened to my gym?'

'It's not your gym,' I said. 'It's our gym and that's the way we like it.'

'For God's sake,' said the PI, 'don't let Lordy get hold of a hacksaw or we'll all be in for it!'

It was funny and all the lads were laughing. But the gym stayed the way we'd made it, which was good.

Of course it was sometimes a bit claustrophobic in the unit because we were all on top of each other, but we all got on so it wasn't that bad. It was hot in the summer on the Isle of Wight and freezing cold in the winter, but we just put up with it.

In the summer months we used to sit outside on the grass to watch the air shows and firework displays. Sometimes I wished I could escape and swim across the water to freedom, but I knew it wasn't possible.

There was another feller in the unit called Wayne who was a funny character. He just used to sleep all day; the only time he came out of his cell was for his meals and then he went back to bed. One day he came out of his cell all dressed up with his earphones on and a flask strapped on his back. I thought I was seeing things. He went out into the yard and started dancing like a robot; it was very strange but funny to watch at the same time. The doctor was called and he had to be taken away to get some help. I heard later he'd admitted to multiple murders.

I was eventually moved from the Parkhurst unit because it closed down. I heard the IRA lads got out during the 1998 Peace Process. I was happy for them regardless of what they'd been involved in; they were a good bunch of lads that got me through some of my time in prison.

Next I was transferred to Whitemoor Prison in Cambridgeshire for four months, but I only lasted one night on normal location. I didn't like it in there and I kicked off big-time. I told them to get the governor down, and that they could have it the easy way or the hard way. I wanted out of that prison.

I was sent to the seg unit the next day and remained there for the full four months. I didn't want to mix with anyone, and I wouldn't comply with their rules or put up with the disgraceful treatment that was dished out. Also, the prison stank like shit.

Yes, I hated being in Whitemoor; every day was like a week and every week was like a year. I was just waiting to be moved. What really pissed me off was that the fucking sex offenders were preparing the food for the whole of the prison. I refused to eat anything they made, living on bread and uncooked food for the whole time I was in there. I just didn't trust the dirty nonces with the food; it was obvious that they were contaminating it.

After four months in that shithole I was sent to the CRC (control regime conditions) unit at Hull. I ended up staying there for two years. Anywhere was better than where I'd just come from.

I attended the pottery and art classes at Hull Prison. The unit was self-sufficient. You had your own kitchen, pantry and food; your own shower rooms and gym; your own laundry room. You were just left alone. There was obviously security watching over you but most of the time things ran smoothly. You were still locked up at night but out of your cell during the day.

It was here that I started having sessions with a trainee psychologist. I remember the sessions very well because she'd always sit down with her knees bent up on the sofa and a short skirt inching up her legs. She seemed very relaxed with me; she was always asking me personal questions and letting me ask her about her personal life. I didn't think there was anything wrong with the sessions until she started avoiding me; I don't know what her problem was or if I'd said anything wrong to her. I just stopped going and thought, *to hell with you then*.

However I was later told by the principal psychologist at the prison that she'd written a report for my forthcoming parole board hearing and it said I'd been manipulative and exploitative towards her.

I couldn't believe it. I profusely denied the allegations and explained that she had opened up to me and let me lead the conversations at our meetings. The psychologist also said Hannah had told her I was very flirtatious. I was quite shocked and explained that I'd never have flirted with Hannah; she wasn't my type at all and she need not have flattered herself like that. I explained that I'd just found it easy to talk to her and thought we got on well, but after a while her mood changed and she started to avoid me. I just didn't understand why Hannah didn't tell me if she had a problem with me. After all, it was her that was the trainee psych, not me. But I was so pissed off with her, and thought, *this is not going to go down too well with the parole board.*

When I asked the principal psych to change her report she declined, so I told her I was going to take her to the British Psychological Society.

'You will get me into trouble,' she replied.

'Now you know just how I feel,' was my response to her.

She didn't comply with the BPS's request to submit the report to them. Furthermore, she ended up leaving her job. That just proved to me how the kind of people the government employ can end up affecting prisoners' lives; unlike the prisoners they have the choice to just move on, or in her case move abroad.

I didn't expect to be paroled, but at the same time I didn't want anything to go into my files that could hinder me further down the line. I was sick of all the bullshit that was written about me. It seemed that no matter what I did to try to get on and better myself, there was always someone dragging me back down.

After being in the Hull unit for two years I was moved out on a security breach because they found a hole in one of the cells. At first we were all put in the seg unit next to the CRC unit for one week, and then back on normal location while the Woodcock team, who police prison rules and regulations, came down to assess the breach. When they'd finished looking in one of the cells they'd made more of a mess and caused more infrastructural damage than the actual hole they found.

John Gainer came down from the CRC committee to see me and the other lads. He came to check if we were alright and also to see that there were not going to be any disturbances. I was told I'd be moved out over the next few days but not placed under any disciplinary order, as he knew I had nothing to do with the alleged attempted breakout while I was in Hull.

A few days later, his colleague John Golds came to visit me and I was moved to Durham Prison. I was in Durham for twenty-eight days. I can remember the first morning I woke up there; I took my bowl to get my breakfast. I always had porridge, but when I went to the server a screw told me they didn't have it in there.

'You what? You must be joking!'

'No, it's a continental breakfast in here,' he replied.

'That's funny, because I didn't know I was on the fucking continent.'

So I told him to put me down to see the governor and also the doctor, who both agreed with me that the food in there was insufficient but couldn't do anything about it. I was told that if I wanted more continental food they'd give it to me; I told them to shove it where the sun don't shine!

I was starving in there and told them I wanted out of their

prison before I starved to death. I started kicking off and getting verbal with the screws. I think they knew I wasn't going to shut up and put up with it, so they arranged for me to be shipped out before things got out of hand. But I had to have the continental breakfast right up to my move otherwise I'd have wasted away.

To this present day, prison food is quite degrading and doesn't equate with dietary requirements. Many a time I've taken the issue up with various dignitaries, including the Queen, from whom I surprisingly got a reply (albeit six weeks after writing), whereas some dignitaries remained indifferent and arrogant.

I was moved to Whitemoor Prison and taken straight to the segregation unit. I was going mad. I told them if they didn't get the governor down I was going to kick-off. I went out in the yard and told the screws I wasn't coming back in until they got John Golds on the phone.

I was pacing around the yard and shouting at the screws, telling them that if they came near me they'd get it. Some of the other lads joined in the stand-off; even though I didn't want them to, they wanted to stand by me.

I soon caught the attention of the governor and he came down to speak to me. I told him John Golds from the Home Office had been to see me and said I wouldn't be placed in the seg unit once I got shipped out of Hull Prison. The governor promised me if I went back into the unit he'd keep to his word and get Golds to come down. I told him to speak to him on the phone first, only then would I go back in.

I waited for a while and the governor came back out,

telling me he'd made a call to John Golds. The governor was a horrible bastard; he was from HMP Leeds which carried the stigma of brutality. He told me I'd be getting a visit on the following Tuesday. I told him I'd go back to my cell because he'd kept to his word and made the call. I told the lads everything was under control and I'd give them till Tuesday to arrange the visit. The promise was kept and John Golds came down to see me. He couldn't believe I'd been messed with and taken back to Whitemoor Prison, which everyone knew I detested.

CHAPTER NINETEEN

GOAD

I was moved to Doncaster Prison the next day and placed on normal location on GOAD (good order and discipline). I wasn't handcuffed and I was escorted in a decent manner, which should have been the case for years by then. It's all a matter of having respect for fellow human beings. I didn't have any problems and the move went well.

When I got to Doncaster I was put in the segregation unit. As I walked past the association room I noticed some faces I knew; I rang a bell and a screw let me out so I could get something to eat. I went back down to the association room and asked the lads how come they were in there: they had newspapers, magazines and the television was on. One of the lads said they were on association and had the freedom to go sit in that room.

'How come they can go into the association room but I can't?' I asked one of the screws.

'It was nothing to do with me,' he said.

I told him I wasn't having it; I should never have been placed in the seg unit in the first place.

I told him I wasn't having people near my cell watching TV and playing board games, laughing and joking, when I was banged up all day. I didn't begrudge the other lads what they were doing, but it was three days before Christmas and they were getting special treatment while I was banged up all through the season. It was just not going to happen. I wasn't on report or punishment and I wanted the same treatment as the other lads in the unit or I wasn't staying in their prison, full stop.

About an hour later two of the directors came to see me, Mr Smith and Mr Manderfield, who I knew from Frankland Prison. They were alright with me and asked what the problem was. I explained that I wasn't going to stay in their prison if I didn't receive the same treatment as the other lads. I knew that anyone on a GOAD move is subject to an executive decision. But I wasn't on any kind of report or punishment, and prison rules clearly indicated I should have access to the facilities of that unit. Some segregation units choose to ignore what GOAD stands for and make their own rules up.

Mr Smith said he'd see what he could do. I told him it was up to them to sort it out.

The next morning they came back and told me they'd changed the rules. From that day on, anyone coming into the prison on a GOAD would have the privileges of the association room and the gym. On that night, 23 December 1996, I was let into the association room.

I remember how on Christmas Day they'd decorated the room and the tables were full of food; there were chocolate logs and trifles, music and board games. I couldn't help thinking how things could have been so different if I didn't open my mouth and stand up for my rights. I'd have been left in my cell all day while this was going on right in front of me. It just proved to me that the system can put things right if it wants to. If we hadn't had an understanding governor, I'd have kicked right off and no one would have had a peaceful Christmas.

And I remember how one of the screws came down to the unit to see me. His name was Matthew and I knew him from another prison; he was alright with me, asking if I wanted to go upstairs on normal location, but I refused. I said I'd have gone on normal location when I first arrived at Doncaster – which I should have done – but they'd put me in the seg unit so I was staying there.

My mate Perry advised me to give it a try; he said I might like it up there. I said I wasn't going unless he was up there too, but he said he was getting out soon. I thought about it for a while and, after some persuasion from Perry, I said I'd go up just for one day to try it out.

When I was up there I walked up to a punchbag that was placed on the wing, and started hitting it. Everyone was looking at me; I didn't like the atmosphere. I told the screw I wanted to go back to the unit; just as I was walking through the gates I heard someone say, 'Who is he, is he a nonce?'

After that I went mad and told the screw to let me back in, but he said, 'Come on, Al, calm down...'

I shouted over to the lads to watch their fucking mouths! I was no nonce and they'd soon find out exactly who I was.

Then I went downstairs and told Perry what had happened. He laughed his head off.

I stayed on the unit for another week until Perry moved out, and then went back upstairs on normal location. It was Perry who'd talked me into giving it another try because he said it'd be a good move for me. And so I ended up on normal location.

Perry was sent to the Hull unit as it'd been reopened. I just got on with it in Doncaster Prison. It ended up alright upstairs; I was asked if I wanted a job painting the walls of the landings when and where required. The wages were good so I said yes.

I also worked in the kitchen for a while, but I said I'd only help out with the cleaning and washing duties if I went on the server, giving out the food. If someone asked for more food they'd get it. I wouldn't deprive anyone because I'd been in other prisons where the food dished out wasn't even enough to feed a mouse.

In fact I worked in the back of the server for quite a while; I enjoyed it. But I still did a lot of complaining, writing letters to all manner of dignitaries. One day I went to put a complaint into the office because of the racism inside the prison. A female screw I gave the letters to looked at me and said, 'Mr Lord, I'm sorry but I didn't know you were black.'

'My father is from Belize in Central America,' I replied, 'and my mother is white Irish.'

I think she thought I was white because I had pale skin

and a shaven head. Being locked up does your skin no good; prisoners deprived of natural sunlight often look grey and pale.

She said that she'd heard about my reputation, and told me her husband was a black man. I asked her how she found it in the prison and she admitted it was very racist. She'd even stopped going to work functions and parties because of her husband's colour, so she could sympathise with me.

One day while I was in the kitchen, the same screw apologised to me in front of the lads. I asked her what she was apologising for, and she reminded me that a few days earlier she'd made a joke about putting me inside the fruit trolley full of bananas. I told her it didn't matter and I'd taken it as a joke, not a racist remark.

But then racial abuse in that prison was a daily occurrence. They would call black or mixed-race prisoners 'coons' or 'niggers'. I got called 'Monkey Man' or 'Monkey Feathers' – which was very strange, considering one of the female screws thought that I was white.

However I didn't have any trouble in there. Most of the inmates were from Barnsley; they were all a bit backward and used to hang about in little groups. When some of the other lads were watching television, a group of Barnsley lads came in and one of them turned the TV to another channel. I wasn't that bothered because I was reading and having a bit of banter at the back of the room, but I knew some of the lads were pissed off. I thought to myself, *I'll remember the fat one's face and get him back some other time.*

Then one day, I walked past the television room and

Fatty was sat there on his own. I went over to the television, changed the channel and stood in front of it.

'What are you going to do about it?' I asked him.

He just got up and walked out.

'Yes, you shitbag! Not so big now without your mates, are you, dickhead?'

I got a visit one day from John Golds, who asked me if I'd like to go on normal location at Long Lartin Dispersal Prison. I said I didn't know and told him I'd think about it. Golds was alright by me. He tried his best to help me along; he was honest and fair and always stuck by his word.

Mr Smith, the director, came down to see me the next day and advised me to try it. If I didn't get on there I could always come back. I think that they thought I was starting to settle down and get on with the time I had to do, walking away from any confrontation with the screws, and it was a step in the right direction for me to move.

They arranged for a governor called McLaughlin and two screws to come from Long Lartin Prison and have a chat with me. I think the governor was surprised that I was calm, unaggressive and listened to what they were saying. But I couldn't believe it when he said to me, 'Just keep taking the pills, lad, and you will be okay with us at Long Lartin.'

I took offence straight away.

'What do you mean? I don't take pills, I don't take any kind of medication, and I don't know why you're insinuating that I need to.'

He apologised and said he'd expected me to be more

164

aggressive; he didn't expect me to be well mannered or intelligent, and just presumed I'd been taking anti-depressants or tranquillisers. They left it with me to decide about the move.

I thought about giving it a go and spoke to the governor about it. After about a week I was transferred to Long Lartin Prison, but when the screws turned up for me there was a problem. They met me at reception and handed me a boiler suit with stripes down it.

'You must be fucking joking,' I told them, 'there is no way that I am putting that on, you can go and fuck off back to where you came from and take that piece of shit with you because I'm not going to your fucking prison in that!'

I was fuming. The security screw from Doncaster started laughing at the screws from Long Lartin because he knew I'd kick-off if they even attempted to get me into that suit. A phone call was made and he said I could travel in my tracksuit.

In fact I was in two minds as to whether I should go with them at first. If that was the way I was going to be treated from the start, how the hell was it going to be when I got there? Then I remembered what the governor said about me being able to come back, so off we went.

I only served around three weeks in Long Lartin. I found it depressing; it was an old prison and everything seemed to be falling apart.

While there I was put on normal location in a cell next to a few lads I knew from various prisons, so I got on with it. Then one day I asked one of the lads what the hell was going on in that prison; I felt like something wasn't right, there was a bit of an atmosphere with some of the inmates.

I found out that F-wing had been closed down and some of the nonces put on normal location on my wing. I was so pissed off, especially when I saw Straffen, the child killer, on my landing. I told him to get off.

What's more I didn't like Long Lartin; it was too dirty for me. There were 'dirty parcels' (shit, that is) being thrown out of the windows; the prison was one big cesspit.

I wanted out. I disobeyed orders and wouldn't go back to my cell during the day to lock down. I started getting verbal with the screws. I knew how to get thrown out of a prison; I'd done it many times before. I knew it wouldn't be long before the control and restraint team would come for me.

One day I was on my landing and one of the nonces walked past me. I started kicking-off, shouting for the screws to get me out of there. It wasn't long before I was escorted to the seg unit.

When I got there, the control and restraint team was waiting for me. One of the screws told me to strip off; I asked him why. He told me that since I'd arrived in Long Lartin, the place had started to deteriorate. I was being moved out.

CHAPTER TWENTY

BRUTALITY
TO THE MAX

They handcuffed me and some of the screws started getting verbal. I was taken by surprise at the sudden move because I thought it'd take much longer to be shipped out.

I was walked straight out to a waiting van. Before I got in, I asked the screws for my box of toiletries but they just laughed at me. I thought, *right*.

So I jumped in the van, locked them out and started smashing the inside up. After about ten minutes, the riot team turned up with their shields and dogs. The governor and the doctor came to the back of the van and tried to get in. One of the CR team jumped up on the step, saying he was going to open the door and take me back to the seg unit. If I didn't comply he was going to let the dogs in.

I heard the door unlock. I didn't move because I didn't

167

want them to have the satisfaction of setting the dogs on me. Two screws got in the van, grabbed hold and pulled me out through the line of screws and riot squad with their shields up and dogs ready to pounce.

As soon as I got thrown in the cell they all piled in. I was rolling all over the floor as they kicked hell out of me. One of the screws went as far as jumping on my testicles a few times. I was handcuffed and couldn't defend myself. Every blow was excruciating and the pain that shot up my back was unbearable. But I didn't want to show them how much pain I was in so I just gritted my teeth.

After they finished beating me to a pulp they left the cell, laughing, and banged the door closed behind them. I was just lying there on the floor. I could not move. I was left in the strip cell for about an hour.

Eventually they returned. As the door was unlocked and I was being moved, I noticed the CCTV camera.

'Hey, scumbags!' I said. 'You were being filmed while you were doing your dirty work on me.'

But I thought to myself that they'd taken the film out, because one of the screws was shaking his head as if to say, *no, we weren't*. I couldn't see them filming that level of violence, not with so many of them attacking me.

Then I noticed a female screw staring at me with a smug smirk on her face. She could clearly see I was distressed and in a bad way, but she looked me up and down like I was a piece of shit.

'Who the hell is fucking you, you ugly bitch?' I said to her. 'He or she must be blind!'

I was brought out of the cell in the body belt and escorted to a van, still getting the odd dig off one of the screws. As I passed the governor I shouted back at him, 'You are the first one I'm going to prosecute when I speak to my brief, you evil bastard!'

The screws grabbed hold of me, tied my legs up tight behind my back and threw me into the strong box inside the van. They put the air conditioning on full blast; I was freezing as I was naked and still in the body belt. I told the screws to turn off the air but they just laughed.

I started kicking at the cage door and managed to get my legs loose. I kicked the cage door harder, looking at the screw at the end of the cage with sheer determination on my face.

'If you don't turn the fucking air-con off I am coming for you, do you understand?'

The look on his face was a picture of sheer terror; he soon had the air-con turned off and I stopped banging.

When we got to Woodhill Prison the door opened and I was dragged out. I couldn't believe there were so many of the control and restraint team there, all lined up on each side of the van like they were waiting for Hannibal Lecter. As soon as my feet touched the ground I ran at them, but I had my body belt on and couldn't get to them.

It is common practice that if a prisoner, for whatever reason, is being 'refractory' and all control measures have been applied but failed, then a transfer is imminent. But the authorities sometimes have the common sense to create an atmosphere of neutrality by not antagonising an already volatile situation. In this case, I found it peculiar that a control and restraint team had followed the transport van and the screws were from Long Lartin Prison. Inevitably, it resulted in physical confrontation.

Once they got hold of me they dragged me to the segregation unit. I was beaten up badly again; they beat me until I could no longer move. Once they'd left I became verbal with the Woodhill screws. However, the acting governor at Woodhill came straight down to see me and expressed his concern at the provocation. I quote:

'Lordy, I don't know what the fuck is going on here!'

He said he'd never seen anyone arrive into his prison in such a state.

I was going mad at him and asked why he'd let this happen to me. He said it was nothing to do with him or his prison. He was not responsible for me being brought there under that much control. I guess they wanted to give me a good sending-off present by sticking the boot in one more time.

As soon as I found out the screws from Long Lartin Prison had left, I settled down. I was taken out of the body belt and put into a cell. I was given a drink and some clean clothes.

I was in Woodhill Prison for four months. I was left alone and treated alright. I just got on with doing my own thing; I was able to get my training into a daily routine. I felt calm and content, and the time seemed to pass without any tension.

I was doing a lot of reading and writing too. I'd had enough of fighting and wanted to serve out my sentence in some kind of peace. I had no idea when, or if, I was ever going to be released, but I never gave up hope and was determined to try my best to change and to beat the system. The system that had taken most of my life away from me.

I wanted one day to get my liberty back. I wanted so much to be on the out, so I could expose what it was really like to live in Her Majesty's prisons.

One of the screws I'd met while in Birmingham Prison said to me one day that he couldn't believe how much I'd calmed down. To him, I didn't seem to be the same person.

I told him I still had all the same issues and values, but I was fed up with conflict and chose to ignore any derogatory remarks from the screws. I'd use a pen as my weapon instead of my fist.

He just looked at me as if I'd gone mad. But I knew exactly what I was doing and that it was the only way I'd ever get out.

I was full of anger and resentment at the prison regime, but I knew I had to change my tactics. I had to learn to play them at their own game. I'd realised I was creating my own calamity, and that realisation can be daunting. But sometimes our principles get in the way.

My conscience had taken a turnaround that would enable me to progress, slowly but surely. It also enabled me to put my energy into writing and doing things the right way. I knew I had to fight for change within the prison system. I also knew I'd helped change the sanitation rules that abolished the slop-out system after the Strangeways demonstration. But there was still a very long way to go.

I knew at first hand that the brutality and abusive behaviour by the screws had not changed one bit. I also knew that, by fighting back while I was inside and taking their bait time and time again, I'd never be released. I'd learned the hard way for a very long time, but the only way I could beat the regime was by getting out of prison fit and alive. So many of them would be pissed off if I was ever released.

But I had to change the way I handled things, to ignore the snide remarks and racial taunts and just agree with whatever was thrown at me. I started putting pen to paper and wrote to whatever dignitaries I felt I had to complain to. I even wrote to the Queen at Buckingham Palace and the Prime Minister at Downing Street, receiving replies that gave me the confidence to carry on.

I got a visit in Woodhill from John Gainer of the Home Office, who said he was concerned about the treatment I'd received in Long Lartin because he'd read some of the letters of complaint I'd sent. He was disgusted with what had happened to me despite all my recent progress. I told him that when I eventually got my toiletries from Long Lartin, the shampoo and toothpaste had been mixed and the others had been bust open. I told him about the antagonism and the level of brutality endured on a daily basis in Long Lartin. He apologised and said he had no idea; but then no one ever does till it's too late.

He felt bad that he'd advised me to move to Long Lartin, thinking my progress and good behaviour would mean better treatment for me. He asked if I wanted to go back to Doncaster Prison; I said I didn't mind because I knew people in there and I liked the gym.

It was soon arranged for me to be shipped out to Doncaster.

While I was getting ready to leave, the governor came to the reception to see me off.

'Good luck, Lordy,' he said out loud. He was very surprised that only a couple of screws were there. As he said to one of the custody officers taking me to Doncaster, 'You should've seen the way Lordy was brought here, I've never seen anything like it in all my years of service. I didn't know what to expect when Lordy was brought out of the cage. Are you sure you're going to be able to handle him?' he asked them.

You should have seen the look on their faces.

'Only joking, lads, Lordy is no trouble,' the governor said. 'Well, that's if you don't get on the wrong side of him.'

He walked away laughing.

CHAPTER TWENTY-ONE

FROM NORMAL LOCATION TO DIRTY PROTEST

I was taken to Doncaster Prison and stayed in the segregation unit for one night. Then I was put on normal location, actually on the same wing as when I was last there. I still had a few mates in there that I was happy to meet up with again. I just wanted to get on with it and get settled into a routine. I knew I'd be there for quite a while, so I wanted to fit in and get through the security categories one by one, so that the gate got that little bit closer to opening for me.

I'd been settled in for quite some time and had a job in the kitchen on the server. I'd kept my head down and out of trouble, but it was short-lived. It all went wrong again when I was in the kitchen and this bully walked in. I'd heard about him. He just walked over to the pantry, took the custard out and started eating it.

So I asked him what the hell he was doing. He got lippy so I went over and punched him in the face. He went down like a lead balloon. I just walked out of the kitchen, went back to my cell and left him there with custard all over his face.

The next day I was sat in the kitchen on the server table. I didn't think it was a problem because I'd seen other inmates sat there. I was talking to some of the kitchen staff when this big, fat, female screw came in and gave me a dirty look, then walked back out. I didn't think anything of it because it went on quite a lot, but apparently she'd told me to get off the table and I hadn't heard her.

As soon as she left the room, one of the other women screws told me to get off the table with an aggressive tone to her voice.

'Why should I get off when every day you lot sit here, what's the difference?' I reasoned.

But I jumped up and went back to my cell. 'Nothing ever changes,' I said on the way out.

That night I got a note put under my door stating that I was going to be put on report and had to go to the seg unit the next morning. I thought to myself, *here we go, I'm off again; just when I thought I was progressing they're dragging me back down.*

I went to the seg unit first thing the next morning and couldn't believe it when I got there. I met up with one of the screws I'd had a lot of trouble with when I was in Wakefield seg. (I actually poured a large pot of porridge over his head.)

I knew my days were numbered in that prison as soon as I saw him there; he had a big smirk on his face.

There was no way I was going to stay there, knowing that from that day one I was going to be stitched up and suffer abuse again. I could only go backwards.

I told another screw that I'd done nothing wrong; I was sitting at the table because other people had sat there before, including the staff, but he wouldn't listen. He said I was going to be staying in the segregation unit for a number of days. I told him I wasn't going to stay in seg and wanted out of the prison.

Then I walked back down the block and a screw tried to grab hold of me. I pushed him away, telling him to get off of me. I wasn't having it. I pushed past the screws, went back in the unit and told the screw in charge it was a deliberate set-up.

'Get someone down to see me because I'm not staying in this prison!'

I went back to the cell and started banging about. The next minute Mr Smith, one of the directors, came down.

'Come on, Lordy, what's going on?' he asked.

I told him I wanted out of his prison. He said he'd heard I'd knocked someone out and I was becoming a nuisance again. He wanted me to meet him halfway, to stay in his prison and sort things out.

'No, I want out.'

After a few minutes of talking to him he said, 'Okay, I don't want any disturbances or uproar here, I will see what I can do.'

'I want out today.'

I was moved that day to Full Sutton Prison in York. I got taken straight down to the segregation unit because of being on report from Doncaster Prison. When I got to the cell I couldn't believe who'd progressed up the ranks to governor; it was a screw I had some trouble with in the past.

'Welcome home, Lordy.' He thought he was being smart. 'I didn't think it'd be long before you came back to us.' He was laughing.

'I didn't stay in your prison for long last time, so let's see how long I last this time,' I told him.

But I couldn't be bothered to kick-off and get moved again. I just had to ignore the remarks and get on with my legal work, writing letters of complaint about the regime and the way the Cat-A system was run. I'd become the voice of many prisoners through my letters.

I stayed at my desk most of the day. It seemed without doubt that there was always some screw I'd had problems with, somewhere in the country, who'd moved up ranks, held a grudge against me and would make my life hell. As if I didn't have enough to contend with!

Later in the day, whilst I was in my cell, some screw started mimicking monkey noises, echoing throughout the segregation unit. Then the other screws joined in and were laughing out loud. I went to my cell door and shouted out to them: 'When this door opens we'll soon see who the man is!' I wasn't let out of my cell that night.

The next day, my mate Frank Burly from Leeds was brought down into the next cell to me. He was well respected both inside the prison and on the out. He also stood up for what he believed in and on many occasions had taken on the regime. But he'd had trouble with the screws and was brought down; they wouldn't leave him alone and were always taunting him.

Frank told me he'd had enough of being bullied. Their never-ending snide remarks and brutality were getting to him, so he decided to go on a dirty protest. I wanted to support him because I knew Frank well, and I wanted to piss them off. He was a nice man and I didn't like the way he was being treated.

It lasted fourteen days. I know it's not very nice at all, to say the least, but a dirty protest causes a disturbance and gets results. They have to block the wing off where the protest is going on for health and safety reasons.

We also started banging on the doors and windows. We made a pact between us that at 12 o'clock every night we'd start and we'd continue banging all night, on the hour, every hour. It continued for a few days, until I changed it to every half-hour. I just thought that if we caused a big enough disturbance it'd piss the other inmates off, and the screws would have more trouble on their hands because the noise was travelling.

The main reason for the protest was to get Frank's mistreatment noted, and then of course I wanted to be transferred. I'd never wanted to go to Full Sutton in the first place.

I continued to bang on my door and window until one of the screws came down to see me. He said if I'd stop the protest he'd sort my move out the next day.

I gave him the benefit of the doubt and stopped banging. I

got my head down and, as soon as it hit the floor, I was out like a light.

The next day, I waited and waited but no one came to see me. I waited until later that day but no one came down. So I started banging on the door and window again.

Later that evening, they came to move me out. It was the fourteenth day of the protest. My door was opened and I was told I was going. I was escorted to the showers by screws in protective clothing. I was caked with shit and must have stunk to high heaven, but that was part of my protest and it made an impact.

Being on a dirty protest is not appealing at all, but it's a necessity. It affects everyone profoundly, checking the screws' derogatory attitude towards prisoners that they display whenever they have to do any daily task involving the serving of food and water to your cell or delivery of your mail.

Apparently a new regulation now permits the authorities to dispose of all prisoners' belongings when they are on a dirty protest, even though few prisoners ever soil their own property as they wrap it in polythene bags and place it out of the way. It's obvious that this new measure is designed to prevent such a protest.

I was given clean clothes, handcuffed and led away to the waiting van. It was a relief to be out of that shithole.

CHAPTER TWENTY-TWO

FROM BRISTOL BULLSHIT TO DONCASTER PRIVATE

I was transferred to Bristol Prison with my small bag of belongings. I had no trouble on the way; in fact, to my surprise it was a very quiet journey. When I got to Bristol there were screws waiting for me with tracksuits and protective pads on their knees and elbows. I'd never seen that kind of attire before. I was escorted straight to the server as they were serving dinner when I arrived. I was tempted to say, 'No need for the fancy dress, lads,' but I kept my mouth shut.

I got something to eat and then I was led to the segregation unit. When I got to my cell, the senior officer said to me, 'There is not going to be any trouble in here is there, Lordy?'

'If you don't cause me any trouble, I won't cause you any trouble,' I told him.

It was left at that and I got on with it. It wasn't that bad in Bristol Prison, and I stayed away from conflict. But I was only there for four months.

The only thing that comes to mind when I think back to that time is when I met a black feller called Anthony in the exercise yard. He was giving it the big 'un, trying to impress me with all his bullshit; he was very talkative and wouldn't shut up. I'd met a lot of inmates over the years who'd try to impress with their cocktails of lies; they'd big themselves up and try to befriend me, but I was having none of it. I was well known within the system and some inmates thought they'd be safe if I carried them under my wing, but I was carrying no one. I was never part of any group or so-called posse. I had my own set of friends who I could trust, and I could count them on one hand.

A couple of days later another black kid came down to the segregation unit. Anthony had been trying to bully him. I went to the window and told him to stop running his mouth off to the kid; of course, he then started running his mouth off at me. I told him to shut up or I'd be coming after him.

I was put into the exercise yard on my own the next day. I didn't mind being on my own, I was sick of all the bullshit and just wanted to move round at my own pace.

A few days later, another black kid came down to the segregation unit who happened to be Anthony's mate. I could hear how Anthony was still stirring things up for the other kid. I went to the window and told him to shut up with his bullshit and stop pissing me off. He'd also been talking to his mate all night at the window and kept me up.

He started getting very verbal with me out of his window. I shouted at him to stop sucking his teeth, and told him to tell his mates about how he was bullying the young inmates in there. I told him he was nothing but a dirty nonce and when I got hold of him I was going to give him a good hiding.

I'd been informed that the gobshite *was* a nonce. If I'd found out earlier I'd never have walked round the yard with him, talking to the dirty bastard. I was so pissed off that he was trying to befriend me, as I'd heard he raped a young girl. Even the screws didn't like him on account of being a cocky little shit.

I managed to get to his cell door the next day and told him to remember my face, because if I ever came across him in the dispersal system I was going to give him a good hiding. I don't care what colour or ethnic origin they are, if they're a child abuser or sex offender they're just dirty cowards.

Later I was told later that Warren, another inmate who was a big guy and could look after himself, had knocked out the nonce in the yard. I was happy about that. The screws had let Warren out knowing that the nonce had been mouthing off about him. I also heard he screamed and cried like a baby when he was being wrapped up in the belt one night for giving it out to the screws. Just before I transferred out, I went to his cell door, opened the hatch and said, 'You're just a little pussy, you scream like a girl!' I told him I knew the strength of him and I was after him.

I got my things together because I was on a move to Doncaster Prison. The same team came to take me back. I was taken to the segregation unit but put on normal location the next day. I remained in Doncaster Prison for six months, carrying on with the same fitness and exercise routine, and the same job working on the server at the back of the kitchen, on cleaning, washing-up and stores duties.

Doncaster was a private prison. The staff were more amiable, it was clean and the food was much better. The wages were also good and I got visits from my mates Joe Murray and Dave Dale. I'd spend years inside with Joe and, when he got out, he and his mate Dave came to visit me from Liverpool no matter which prison I was in.

I just kept my head down; I was in good spirits, feeling less tension and headaches. There wasn't much going on in Doncaster Prison. Sometimes it could get a bit monotonous and boring, but I couldn't have it all ways.

I met a couple of inmates from the dispersals and had a bit of banter to pass the time. I only had one bit of conflict with a screw who was checking up on me all the time; even when I was asleep in my cell he'd come and bang on my door as if I was on suicide watch.

Being woken up in the middle of the night was something I hated, as I had to be up in the early hours of the morning for my workout. I think he was just doing it to wind me up, so one night, when I heard a knock on my door, I shouted to the screw to fuck off or I was coming for him.

I found out the next night when they came on duty that it was a female screw the night before, and that I'd frightened her.

'You should've seen her face, I think she was shaking in her boots.'

The screw on duty was laughing, but I felt bad. I'd never have shouted and said what I said if I'd known it was a woman – but on the other hand, I'd probably have shouted at anyone who woke me up in the middle of the night.

I just got on with my legal paperwork, writing to the board of governors, the Home Office and various other authorities about the problems I'd encountered throughout my incarceration.

I knew my time was nearly up when I was asked how I felt about a progressive move back to Frankland Prison. It was food for thought. A few years earlier I'd never have thought I'd be looking to the future with a view to getting out of prison. I always thought someone somewhere would stop that from happening.

CHAPTER TWENTY-THREE

FOUR MORE YEARS IN FRANKLAND

About a week later I was shipped out once again, but this time it was on a progressive move. I ended up staying in Frankland Prison, Durham, for four years. It seemed to go very fast.

When I first got there I was very surprised when I was led down to the prison. I asked one of the screws where I was going and he said, 'You are on the new side, all the nonces are in the old part of the prison now.'

What's more I was shocked to hear just how many there were: 420 sex offenders on the old wings. I was put on G-wing on induction for two days. The first person I met up with was Ollie Brady. I knew Ollie from Garth Prison; it was good to catch up and see he was well. He thanked me for my support for him while on the roof at Strangeways.

Ollie had always protested against his sentence and tried endlessly to prove his innocence and to clear his name. I was convinced he was innocent as I'd never seen anyone protest so consistently.

I didn't like the induction much; the same old routine was becoming very tedious. I was called to the office to see the officer in charge. Everyone seemed to fear him but I wasn't going to let anyone intimidate me.

In any case, I think he knew my reputation and just wanted to flex his muscles. When I walked into his room he was sat behind his desk with arms folded and hands under his armpits to make them look bigger. He had his shoulders back and his chest stuck out. He looked me up and down.

'Why are you here?' he asked.

'Why are *you* here?' I replied as I sat down.

He looked at me and shook his head. I found this amusing and rather pathetic. I was sat there listening to him go on about the prison rules and regulations, but I didn't pay any attention. He soon got the message that I was old school and wasn't interested. He also found out that intimidation doesn't work on everyone, especially me.

The next morning I bumped into the same officer and handed him my legal letters to be posted out. He gave me another dirty look.

'Why do have you so many letters?' he asked.

I told him I had permission to have thirty letters sent out to various dignitaries if I wanted to. Further, I told him my letters had nothing to do with him and all he had to do was post them.

He walked past my cell after dinner. 'I am not frightened of you, Lord,' he told me, popping his head round the door.

I just laughed at him and told him to go and do one. After that he left me alone.

Later I found out that some of the other screws wound him up before I even arrived at Frankland. They kept saying to him, 'Lordy is on his way and you need to watch out, Lordy can get very violent with prison officers. He's not fearful of anyone.'

No wonder he was acting like a dickhead. I was moved off the wing later that day and onto F-wing.

While I was on F-wing I had a bit of trouble with a new screw who accused me of covering the Judas hole on my door, when it was already like that before I was put in there. He tried to get me nicked for it so I was kicking off, telling them they could still lift the flap up if they wanted to check up on me. I told Peter Fury – Tyson Fury's nephew, a good friend I'd first met in Frankland – that I was going to do that screw in for telling lies and having me placed on report, but he said to leave it because it'd just land me in more trouble. I wanted to have a clean slate for my next parole board hearing but it seemed the screws were trying their utmost to block my way out.

I was sent down to the seg unit for questioning, but it was by one of the old governors who could see it for what it was. I was sent back to normal location and to my cell – though I had nothing in there as usual, except for my sheet and toiletries.

One day I was sat on the floor in my cell as the door

opened. One of the screws came in and introduced himself as my personal officer. I told him to get out of my cell and that I didn't require a personal screw. He'd come from Long Lartin Prison and he was called Kosminski. I remembered him from the segregation unit, where I was mistreated badly and endured a high level of brutality. He shook his head and left my cell, locking it behind him. Kosminski didn't bother me again; he must have known I hadn't forgotten about the way I was treated in Long Lartin and stayed away from me.

Later on, I was coming up for a general report and he wrote a note saying he didn't think I should be on enhanced status with more privileges, more time out of my cell, more gym time and learning facilities, better food and more visits from friends and family. According to him, if I didn't get my own way I'd resort to violence as I was violent towards prison officers on a daily basis.

I was pissed off about that and requested to see Governor Robson, who was old school. I showed him the report, he couldn't believe it either.

'You're not like that at all, Alan. It is utter nonsense, if you were as this report states you wouldn't be here.' he said.

'I know that, he's just trying to stitch me up!'

Governor Robson told me to leave it with him and he'd sort it out.

I knew I was going to be in Frankland Prison for a long time because that was their way of monitoring me. I was sent there on a progressive move to prove I could remain stable and avoid conflict. I joined in the art and design classes with my mate Tony Erdmann from Salford, doing contemporary artwork with acrylic paints; I also attended pottery classes. The lady who ran the workshop was quite old but she was alright.

But I knew some of the screws had it in for me. Most of the time it came down to the Strangeways riots. No matter which prison I was incarcerated in, I was constantly reminded about the riots in some way or other. After a while I wouldn't talk to the screws in there. I wrote signs on my hands: my left hand had 'NO' written on it and my right hand 'YES'.

The only one of them I spoke to in the rest of my four years was Bob Cousins. I'd known Bob for over twenty years, having first met him in the early 1980s. I even requested him to be my personal officer. He was a gentleman who did his job professionally and considerately. During the first Strangeways Prison trial he attended as a character witness for me, even though he was still a serving prison officer.

I was grateful to Bob Cousins because he had the courage to stand up for me against all odds. I can honestly say that, out of all the years I was in prison, he was the only screw I had any kind of respect for. He understood me and always had time to listen to my concerns about the politics of the regime. Bob would even come to talk to me when he was on night duty, as I was up at the crack of dawn for circuit training.

Time seemed to go by quite quickly. When Tony and I passed all our art exams we were told we didn't need to go back to the classes anymore. I was pissed off because we'd enjoyed the classes, it gave us something to look forward to and it was good to be able to use our creativity. It was kind of therapeutic, but it was sprung on us on at the last minute that we could no longer attend. The woman who ran the classes told us they were for the purpose of passing an exam, probably to make the prison statistics look good. If we'd have known that we'd have failed our exams to stay and do them all over again.

I was walking back through the yard, after speaking to the art teacher, when I bumped into Mr O'Brian, who was one of the five governors of the prison, and a bright red-faced screw we used to call Tonka Toy, because he thought he was unbreakable. I told the governor what had happened to us:

'Surely they can't just drop us like that when it's part of our routine?'

He told me to leave it with him and he'd see what he could do.

I called back into the office the next morning. I couldn't believe it when the governor told me we had our places back on the arts-and-crafts course. You should have seen the art teacher's face when Tony and I walked in.

'We're back!'

The education officer came to see me. Beryl was nice, I knew her from when I was last in Frankland Prison. She told me she'd heard what had happened in the art class and was happy things were sorted out.

Then one of the principal officers came over and offered me a painting job. He was looking for someone to paint the walls on the wings. I took the job offer but it only lasted one week as there wasn't enough work. Instead I got a job as a gym orderly; I'd always worked out and enjoyed circuit and weight training, so it was a bonus for me.

I felt good about myself and had a different outlook on my future. I liked bodybuilding and weight training; it was good for my wellbeing. It was my kind of medication. I didn't need drugs or alcohol to get through the day; as long as I got my gym fix I was okay.

Plus I was thinking I could open my own gym if I ever got out. I'd taken some exams for health and safety and got on well with like-minded people. I felt calm and kept busy with my legal work. I was focused on going through the security categories without any problems.

After spending four years with Tony Erdmann, he was getting ready to be released and go home. I was happy for him, but at the same time I was going to miss him because we spent a lot of time together. We used to have a laugh, exchange banter and take the piss out of the screws. We also spent a lot of time in the gym, studied and worked together, so I felt a bit low knowing he was no longer going to be around.

I was getting a bit agitated after Tony had gone so they made a decision to transfer me out. I got a move to Dovegate Prison in Uttoxeter. I felt better knowing that I was going to be in different surroundings, but at the same time I didn't want to go to a shithole either.

We stopped off at Full Sutton segregation unit overnight. The atmosphere at Full Sutton was very tense. Myself and an inmate named Jerry Hamilton from Jamaica got transferred at the same time; we were confined to the old seg unit and, inevitably, screws I'd encountered still harboured their resentment towards me.

It was made obvious the following morning in reception, just before I was leaving. A security officer was being smart.

'I remember when we had Lord in here before – he was a handful, weren't you, Lord?' he remarked. 'You caused a lot of trouble and chaos the last time you were here.'

He looked straight at me. I think he was just testing me to see how I'd react.

'You've lost some weight, haven't you, Lord?'

'Maybe I have, but I can still handle myself.'

'You're off to a Cat B, are you?'

'Yes, and I bet you never thought I'd be heading to a Cat B, did you? It must've come as some surprise, eh?'

He looked pissed off. He was just a knob who thought that, because the number on his blouse was 007, he was working for Her Majesty's Secret Service, not working in Her Majesty's Prisons.

'To be honest, Lord, I never thought you would make it out of Cat A.'

'Well,' I replied, 'I was shaken, but I was never stirred.'

CHAPTER TWENTY-FOUR

A BOGUS AFFAIR

I was handcuffed to one of the security officers and off I went to Dovegate, a private prison. When I got to Dovegate there was a bit of confusion because they didn't know if I was going onto normal location or on the therapeutic community unit. I told them I wasn't going on TC as it was full of people with personality disorders and nonces.

The lifer team came down to see me and arranged for me to go on normal location. Dovegate was a clean and tidy prison. When I was sorted out, had taken everything I could out of there, and did my usual bleach and clean, I was able to paint my cell – which was a first for me. I painted it chocolate brown; it looked just like a chocolate factory.

There was a wooden bed frame in my cell but it was bolted down and I couldn't take it out. I didn't want to start any disruptions so I just left it there. People thought I was mad because I still slept on the floor and kept everything to the bare minimum, but I was always going to live out my time in the system that way. It was my protest about the treatment I'd endured throughout my imprisonment and it wasn't going to change, no matter how far down the line I'd come.

The food was alright in Dovegate too. I just got on with my legal paperwork, challenging the authorities on their wrongdoings and mistreatment. I carried on with my gym and circuit training; we got twelve hours outside so I was training in all kinds of weather, which was good. I was also working as a gym orderly and built myself back up.

I met a lad called John who I thought was going to be a bit of a nuisance, as he sucked his teeth at me one day when I walked passed him and his mates. I pulled him aside and asked him what he thought he was doing; he just put his head down.

But despite that he ended up being a good mate, as he was into the gym and fitness. John was a character I came to respect, regardless of our first encounter.

I recall our first sports day event: we had a bike race, my first ride in many years, and it was like *Wacky Races*. One of the lads went so fast that he couldn't stop and almost ran into one of the others, but ended up going right into the wall. My stomach was killing me I was laughing so much.

In fact I ended up in Dovegate Prison for nine or ten months. It was okay. I only had one altercation, with an inmate called Simpson who I think was a bit of a fruitcake; he certainly had a big mouth and bad attitude. One day I was in the gym and he walked over while I was sat talking to Hannah Thomas, a female screw. He just stood staring at me. I ignored him and carried on talking to her but he butted in.

'Don't interrupt me when I'm talking,' I told him.

'You can talk to her in your cell,' he said.

I wasn't having his snide remarks, so I told him to get in *his* cell so we could sort it out. He said okay, so off we went. I told a screw I passed on the stairs not to press the riot button and to turn a blind eye. He nodded.

We bounced around his cell, knocking holes out of each other till I got the better of him and knocked him flying over his chair. I just walked out, telling him to keep his big mouth shut in the future and to stay away from me in the gym.

I found out later he was jealous over Hannah, the screw I was talking to, because she'd come on to me in a big way. Rumours were flying round the wing about an affair between Hannah and I. Apparently she'd been talking to Simpson before talking at great length, and getting flirtatious, with me.

It all started when I was sat at my desk outside my cell, where I always wrote. One day Hannah brought my letters over; I said thanks but I didn't lift my head up to acknowledge her. She asked me who the letters were from. I told her they were from a psychic medium I was writing to.

'You don't believe in all that crap, do you?' she asked.

'Don't knock it till you try it,' I answered.

I told her I was very sceptical but interested at the same time. Then she came over, leaned her bottom on my chair and said, 'You are doing my head in.' I was a bit taken aback.

'What do you mean?' I didn't know what was going on but I had a feeling something was wrong with her.

'You never look at me or talk to me, you don't give me eye contact or even acknowledge me. It's driving me mad, I haven't slept for three weeks.'

I thought she might be frightened of me because of my past.

'Look,' I said, 'to quash any fears you may have of me I'll talk to you from time to time, so you can see I'm not like what they say I am. But don't think for one minute I'll give the time of day to any other screw in here.'

She smiled and said, 'Okay, that's good.' It did cross my mind then that she was coming on to me, but I was unsure if it was some kind of set-up because I knew she had a boy-friend among the screws.

Hannah was fit, young and pretty, with olive skin; I think she was half-Greek. I felt flattered that she'd taken a liking to me; it made me feel good to have some female attention and the thought crossed my mind that I should get into her. I'd always wanted to fuck a female screw, just to put one over on the regime, but most are as ugly as sin.

I got up from my desk. She brushed past me, looked into my eyes and smiled. I smiled back and said I'd see her tomorrow. Then I went in my cell to bang up early, as I did every night.

When my intercom went I was fast asleep. When I answered it a female voice said, 'It's me, Hannah, come out and talk to me on the landing.'

I was surprised but excited at the same time. She was

talking for ages, telling me about how she wasn't happy in her relationship, asking me personal questions about my past, if I had a girlfriend on the out or if I liked any of the other female officers.

To be honest, I liked what I was hearing. I told her there was no woman in my life, that I was very young when I got sentenced and I'd never found any of the female screws attractive. I was thinking it could be the start of something interesting, something stimulating.

After talking to her for a while, I went back to my cell and got my head down. My imagination was running wild and I was thinking all kinds of things. It could have been a set-up but maybe it was someone who genuinely took an interest in me, and it'd been quite some time since I had any female attention so I was hoping it was the latter.

I hadn't been in bed long before I heard a rustling at my door. I looked round and there was a note passed underneath it. It was from Hannah, saying: 'I want you, I want you bad.' She said how much she wanted my body wrapped around hers. I couldn't believe it; I'd had no idea she felt that way about me.

All sorts of sexual fantasies were rushing through my mind that night. I hoped no one would look through the spy hole and catch me doing the five-finger shuffle.

The letters continued for quite some time, getting more provocatively sexual; some of her words were very explicit and let my imagination run wild. One day she put a pair of her knickers in my hand while I was talking to her. It was very pleasing to say the least, but I wanted the real thing.

All the flirting on the landing and the exchange of sexual banter had to go to the next level. It was very frustrating for me not to be able to grab her and stick my tongue in her mouth.

I felt like a dog on heat all the time. One day, when I got back from the gym, she was looking me up and down and talking about how she wanted to touch my body and feel my muscles, but couldn't in front of the other inmates.

Next I noticed the lads talking about how long she'd been talking to me. I knew some of them had tried to get into her in the past and had been knocked back; some were even getting jealous and starting with the banter, but I just brushed it off. I didn't want to admit to anyone, including myself, that I had feelings towards her. I guess anyone would in my position. It's not unusual for liaisons of this nature to occur up and down the prison system, and I neither condone nor disapprove.

It's inevitable that, since the introduction of females into an all-male environment rife with sexual frustration, boredom, tension and Neanderthal testosterone, instinct will take over at any given opportunity. Unfortunately, the prisoner may suffer the consequences whereas a female on a sexual quest can walk away from the prison confines. The prisoner may have to endure solitary confinement for months, with loss of privileges and progress, while also running the gauntlet of resentful screws. Someone once said to me they felt most female screws were there to take advantage of an all-male prison by being provocative slags on a power trip.

That day I felt a bit on edge because of all the looks we

were getting. I told her I had paperwork to do, and that I'd catch up with her later.

I later heard from one of the lads that some prick called Johnston had started rumours about Hannah and I, so I went up to his cell to tell him to stop spreading shit about her.

He said she used to come and talk and she was prick-teasing him before I'd started talking to her. I said I wasn't stopping her from talking to him; if he wanted to talk to her, go ahead. But equally, if Hannah didn't want to talk to him anymore it was nothing to do with me; if he had a problem, he should take it up with her.

One day, as I came in from the exercise yard after circuit training for a shower, I was ascending the stairs as Hannah was coming down at the same time. It came to mind that in one of her letters she'd written how she wanted me to put my lips to hers, so I said to her: 'Get back up those stairs and go in your office.'

She immediately did a U-turn into the office, but when I put my arms around her to kiss her she brushed me away fast. She said she heard someone coming close to the office, but I didn't know if that was an excuse because I didn't hear anything. She asked me to leave the office right away, which of course I did.

Things started to come to a standstill with Hannah. I wanted to put her to the test to see if she really wanted me as much as she kept telling me in her letters and notes, which by now numbered thirty-seven. I came up with the idea of contacting my mate Tony; I asked him to phone the prison and pose as a solicitor, arranging a visit for the following week when I knew Hannah would be on duty and she'd be able to escort me through the various rooms to the visiting area. I knew one of the small rooms we had to go through had no security cameras and we could get intimate with each other there.

Everything went according to plan and the visit was booked. I didn't say anything to Hannah because I wanted to surprise her. In the meantime she opened up even more to me, telling me of the horrible relationship she was in and how her boyfriend mistreated her, beating her or calling her a 'tart' or a 'prison whore'. She told me she wanted to end the relationship but was too scared to move out and needed someone like me to feel secure with.

I should have read between the lines. I was even warned off her by one of the old-school inmates, who told me he could see right through her and she was playing me like a fool. But I wanted to give her the benefit of the doubt and find out for myself.

The day of the bogus solicitor's visit soon came round. I'd been telling Hannah how much she turned me on and how I wanted her up against the prison walls. She was all smiles, sticking her chest out towards me and saying she couldn't wait to feel me inside her.

I really thought that was it, I was actually going to get my leg over Hannah. Even though I had respect for her at the time, I felt like I'd be putting one over the regime by fucking a female officer.

On the morning of the visit I got myself prepared and all spruced up, smelling nice and fresh. Hannah came to take me over to the visitors' room with a big smile on her face. I asked her if she'd missed me during the night and started some sexual banter to test the water. She was like her usual self but seemed more reserved and tense as we walked along the wing.

We had to go through two doors and rooms with security cameras. In between the main ones was a small room with enough space to get intimate. I thought this would be my chance. I felt as horny as fuck watching her arse move from side to side.

When it came to the crunch she backed off. If anything was going to happen, it would have right there. But when I put my arms around her to kiss her, she moved out of the way and shrugged me off.

'What are you doing?' she asked me, walking fast towards the other door.

'I guess I just got played, well done,' I told her.

She put her head down and walked back with a sheepish look on her face. I sat for a while and waited for my pretend solicitor to arrive. I felt so stupid. I just couldn't get my head around what she was playing at, or what she got out of leading me on.

Someone else took me back to my cell. I was pissed off with myself for falling for her lies; she must have got a kick out of playing with inmates' emotions. Well, she got a gold medal from me for being the biggest prick tease I'd ever known. I had thirty-seven letters and a pair of her knickers to prove it.

I avoided her as much as possible, and vice versa. A few

days later I was sat in my cell, trying to sleep, and the music from upstairs was doing my head in. It was coming from that prick Johnston's cell. I went up to tell him to turn the music down and we got into an argument.

'Well what about you and Hannah?' he asked me.

'What's this got to do with Hannah?'

The next minute his mate came to the cell door. I turned round to him and said, 'Give us a minute.' As I turned back round, Johnston jumped on me, called me a 'fucking black bastard' and started punching me.

I got hold of him and threw him to the floor. As he got to his feet I punched him in the head. He went flying, landed on top of his stereo and it broke into pieces. I guess I got two birds with one stone.

At this point a group of lads came around the cell door. He crawled under the table and wouldn't get out. I was trying to grab him and kick him out from under the table, but the other lads were telling me to leave it before the screws came. I told him to keep his fucking big mouth shut and went back down to my cell.

One of the lads came down straight after me and told me Hannah had gone over to Johnston's cell to find out what was going on. He told her he'd had a fight with me over her; other screws had overheard him say it and had gone to inform the governor.

The next minute the screws were stood at my door to take me down to the seg unit. They said the governor wanted to see me about the fight.

Johnston was already there. The governor asked me what

was going on and I told him I'd gone to his cell to ask him to turn his music down. I was sick of his loud music day-in and day-out.

'Yes, I did give him a good hiding,' I admitted.

But in mitigation, I explained to the governor that I wasn't prepared to tolerate reverberating music twenty-four/seven and had no alternative other than to address the matter. I'd never normally lay the blame on a fellow prisoner, whatever the provocation might be. But I wasn't going to listen to that music every day and all night and get ignored when requesting it to be turned down a notch.

'It came to blows, but what can I say other than do what you will?' I told him.

Surprisingly, he was sympathetic and almost praised my action. He gave me three months in the segregation unit but suspended it because he could see my point of view.

I was waiting to be taken back when one of the lifer team said they were moving me to E-wing because of the problems.

'What problems?'

'We heard you've been having an affair with Hannah.'

'No,' I said, 'I haven't been having an affair with Hannah at all.'

I told them they had it all wrong; they said they'd spoken to Hannah and she confirmed we had something going on; they also said things about me that could only have come from Hannah.

So I told them to wait a minute; I went to my cell and got the letters from Hannah, all thirty-seven of them, with another envelope containing her knickers.

'If you're going to do me then do me, but if not I'll go back to my cell,' I told them.

They were shocked at some of the contents of the letters and told me no further action would take place. Hannah had already resigned from her job.

Even though I was played like a fool, I still missed the attention and the cat-and-mouse game she played with me. I felt like I could never trust a female again, because it wasn't the first time a female screw had come on to me and switched it round, and it probably wasn't going to be the last. The finger had been left pointing at me while she just walked away from it all.

I put it behind me and got on with things. But after a few weeks I bumped into Hannah's boyfriend. I'd heard he'd told one of the other screws that I was making everything up, and that it was *me* who was trying it on with *her*.

So I went over to him and said, 'Listen, I don't normally talk to screws like you, but I need to talk to you like a man.'

I told him he'd been played just as much as I had, and he knew what I was talking about. I told him about what had gone on and he looked shocked. I went to my cell and brought him all the original letters, plus a tape recording of the meeting with the lifer team when I was told about the confession from Hannah. He thanked me for being honest and I went back to the gym.

Later that week the lifer team came down and asked me why I'd spoken to Hannah's boyfriend.

'Well, why not, when everyone in here, including the screws, is laughing at him behind his back?'

They said that, thanks to my exposing the letters, he'd taken sick leave.

'It's nothing to do with me if he can't keep his bitch on a leash,' I replied.

I knew my days there were numbered and, to be honest, I was glad to get away. The lifer team came back to see me a few days later and told me I was moving to Kingston Prison.

CHAPTER TWENTY-FIVE

MOVING ON TO KINGSTON

Kingston was a small prison. There were 190 men, all serving life. I was transferred via a night stop at Winchester, which was a dirty shithole. They tried to put me in a cell that was doubled up but I refused; I told them I'd never done so in the past and wasn't going to double up in their dirty prison. Time was getting on and they didn't want any problems, so they found me a single cell.

No sooner had I entered the cell than an inmate came to the door, asking for a roll-up. I couldn't oblige but once I told him I didn't smoke, he said, 'I know you, feller, I'm sure I do. Fuck me, it's Lordy, isn't it?'

He was excited, asking me all kinds of questions. I thought, *God help me, it's the Spanish Inquisition*. I didn't know who the hell he was, but he made me laugh.

In the cell I sat up all night in a chair, as I wasn't going to sleep on the filthy floor. It soon started to get light and I did my workout before they came to take me for breakfast, which was disgusting. The only thing that compensated for that shithole was the view from the window. It was of the River Humber and the surrounding buildings. I'd always seemed to have a window facing a wall, without a view, so it was good to actually see the river and the boats were fascinating.

I was soon on my way to Kingston Prison. While I was waiting to be moved into a holding cell, a lady governor came to see me and asked me how my overnight stay was. I just said it was okay; I couldn't be bothered to slag her prison off. It was her that had to stay in that shithole, not me. But she was alright with me, very chatty. She'd heard all about me, how I'd served a very long time and was doing well on the progressive moves. She wished me luck and went on her way.

I went to reception to check out and was placed in the van that took me to Kingston Prison. When I arrived I immediately recognised one of the officers, it was Ginger Jason from Parkhurst.

'Now then Ginger!' I called to him in my best Liverpool accent.

'Fancy you being here, Lordy! Who would ever have envisaged that?'

'I know, tell me about it.'

'Times do change, Lordy, people move on and get too old to be bothered with all the crap.'

He said someone from security had come down to have a word with me, so I went into a room with a senior officer.

'Listen Lord,' he said, 'you have come to us on a transfer and I will be frank with you, I have heard all about you and I do not want any trouble in here. Do you understand? Because the minute you start in here, Lord, you are out. I will have no one messing about in my prison.'

I just sat listening to him go on with himself.

'I know you have come here on a progressive move but I will not tolerate any nonsense from you.'

'Let's get something straight right now,' I told him. 'I appreciate your pep talk but don't ever talk down to me; I've moved on from any conflict, otherwise I wouldn't be here.'

'I am not talking down to you, Lord,' he insisted.

'Well it's your whole manner and the way you're conducting yourself that I find aggressive.'

He explained that he wanted nothing more than for me to settle in his prison and change my pattern of behaviour. I told him I'd appreciate it if he lowered the tone of his voice so that it was more neutral, then we'd not get off to a bad start. He agreed and apologised. I told him there was no need for an apology and I wasn't there to cause any trouble.

'Well, I hope you settle in well and wish you all the best in Kingston.'

It was a very weird induction. I didn't know what to make of it.

I was taken to A-wing and went into my cell. I got rid of everything inside, which was part of my ritual as everyone who'd heard of me in prison knew. I emptied my cell and bleached it down from top to bottom. I was very clean and I liked my surroundings to be the same.

The layout at Kingston was something I liked, because the gym had ready access and the library was within easy reach. The workshop was at the end of C-wing and I got a job there, recycling cat's eyes and old floodlights for roads.

When I first started I was having a bit of banter with the guys who ran the workshop, Craig and Clive, when one of them said to me: 'Oh Alan, we've heard all about you! We've been a bit anxious about you working in here – you're not going to attack us, are you?'

I just started laughing. 'It's all rumours, you have nothing to worry about – that's if you don't get my back up!' I gave him an evil look; he didn't know how to take it. 'I'm only joking!' I reassured him.

'Good job,' he said, 'I was quaking in my boots.'

And that's how it went on with the banter and jokes. I think the guys liked me in the workshop; Clive got my sense of humour and offered me a cleaning job with more pay, which I enjoyed. It was a very trustworthy job and I ended up having the run of the place. I was trusted to go into cupboards and drawers, and to work with various stocks, which was good when the orders came in thick and fast from the lads. And it was extra pocket money for me! I was on a roll, and my chocolate stash was getting bigger and bigger.

I was in the workshop for quite a long time. I once found some old books dating back to the eighteenth century; some were poetry and some were religious. I found them in an old box and kept them with me for a while but left them when I moved on. (I wish I still had them now, I bet they're worth something.)

And I also remember there was a fire exit stairwell leading up to a large window at the top of the workshop; I used to enjoy just sitting there, looking out onto the harbour at Portsmouth. I'd see people walking past and sometimes they'd look up and wave. I would wave back. I used to wonder where they were going and how they were living their lives. I sometimes felt a bit envious of the normality in front of me, just outside the window on the streets below. I got lost in thoughts of freedom many times and my mind would drift away, but I knew I'd soon have to go back down the stairs, back down to my own world.

I had no major hiccups in Kingston. The screws in there were not that bad and just left the lads alone to get on with their daily routine on the wings. We were all lifers and all in the same boat. I also liked the gym in Kingston. We had sports competitions and in the summer months outdoor activities, like tug-of-war with large ropes, weightlifting and pedal-bike competitions. One of the lads went too fast on his bike and the wheel buckled; he went flying over the handlebars and crashed it. All the other lads were laughing their heads off.

Plus I also met a feller called Paul Eaton from Liverpool, who's still a good friend today. He worked in the kitchen, was a good laugh and a very good cook. He used to cook me buns every Friday and put jam or cheese in them.

Another lad, Frank, had a pet cockatoo; one day I dropped into his cell and Frank said, 'Don't get too close, Al, he'll attack you!'

'Don't be daft, I'll be okay,' I replied.

I went over and started tapping on the cage. The cockatoo went mad and Frank started laughing. The bird flew out of the cage and latched its beak onto my nose. I don't know who was flapping more, me or the bird! All I know is I had a red nose for days.

It was a good atmosphere in Kingston, because it was what it was. All of us just got on with it. The seasons came and went and we got through it as best we could. We made the best out of a bad situation, especially at Christmas. Me, Paul, and two of the other lads used to have a Christmas party. One of them, a lad named Brian, made the best chocolate Eccles cakes ever; he was a baker on the out. I used to eat all the pork pies before anyone else could get their hands on them, smothered in mayonnaise.

Time seemed to go fast. I was quite successful in Kingston in terms of controlling my behaviour, proving that the screws were the cause of my rebelliousness. It had started the very first day that I was cracked across the head in Strangeways, when I was nineteen. I was not going to have them attacking me whenever they felt like it. I had to fight back and stand up for myself, because I'd known I was in prison for the long haul.

But I'd got on well in Kingston and started to think more about getting out and going home. The only thing that was holding me back was not doing the courses, because I just didn't think they were viable. There was the offending behaviour course, the ETS (Enhanced Thinking Skills) course and the CALM (Controlling Anger and Learning to Manage it). I only did two courses (ETS and CALM) out of the six that were put before me because I didn't feel they had any connection to my original crime. They seemed nonsensical and childish, another way for the regime to manipulate prisoners.

I still moved through the categories and it didn't make any difference to my behaviour or my progress. I proved it when I was sent out of Kingston on a progressive move to a Cat-C prison.

While I was in Kingston I went on two parole board meetings, but I knew I wouldn't get parole. It's not that I didn't crave my freedom; I just came to know how the system worked inside and out, and that they didn't want me to be free!

I was happy just to get on with the progressive moves and work my own way out. In my way I wanted to prove to the system that it's not always necessary to do the courses to progress; it's the change in your behaviour and attitude, and being treated with respect as a human being, that will make you a better person.

The first time I was up for parole in Kingston, a journalist called Eric Allison from *The Guardian* attended the parole board meeting. Afterwards he put an article in the paper about the outcome:

At the beginning of May 2010, I travelled to Kingston Prison in Portsmouth to act as an observer at the parole hearing of life-sentence prisoner Alan Lord. It was an interesting experience, which gave me an unexpected insight into the lifer system. I cannot say I was impressed.

Long-time *FRFI* [*Fight Racism! Fight Imperialism!*]

readers will know that Alan was present for 23 of the 25 days of the Strangeways uprising in April 1990. After the revolt he received an additional 10 years in prison sentenced to run concurrently with the life sentence he was already serving.

Alan was 20 years old when he was given life for murder of a jeweller in Manchester in 1981. The trial judge recommended he should serve 15 years. Now, 26 years on, Alan is still a Category B prisoner; having been finally downgraded from the highest security category, Category A, in 2003.

After Strangeways Alan was shunted around the system like a parcel and suffered at the hands of the staff that were not prepared to forgive him for his part in what was the biggest disturbance in British penal history. However, for at least 10 years, he has been a 'model prisoner', and receives good reports from those in daily contact with him.

Despite this general good behaviour, Alan is still seen as something of an awkward customer by the prison authorities. He is not slow to complain but always does so through the official channels. Over the years, he has acquired habits and traits that are seen by his keepers as non-conformist. For example, he does not sleep on a bed – legacy from the days when he was moved (and abused) on a regular basis. He takes the view that the less he 'takes' from those in power, the less they are able to take from him. Using the same reasoning, Alan has never had a television in his cell. He keeps his possessions neatly packed at all times, ready for any sudden move.

A fair-minded system might view such traits as idiosyncrasies, understandable pockets of behaviour after a quarter of a century of incarceration. Observing the parole hearing, it became clear that the system did not share that outlook.

A district judge chaired the hearing, and a governor was there to present the views of the Secretary of State. A barrister represented Alan and there were several staff witnesses from Dovegate, his previous prison and Kingston.

The board heard that Alan was employed at Kingston, that he was on enhanced status and was a 'polite' prisoner, who did not present any concerns. Then, a lifer governor from Dovegate said that Alan had impressed there as well, but issues had arisen as a result of a relationship between him and a female custody officer. It was agreed by all concerned that this relationship had been entirely mutual; however, as soon as it came to light the work Alan was doing with a female psychologist was immediately terminated and it became apparent that his days at that prison were numbered.

Astonishingly, both the governor and the psychologist spent an inordinate length of time discussing whether Alan was 'institutionalised' or, 'too rigid in his thinking'. They were concerned that, if Alan was downgraded to Category C or D he might have difficulty in sharing a cell after being so long on his own, as if sharing a tiny space in a prison with another man somehow proved a lesser degree of 'institutionalisation'. It was even put to him that by not watching television he was lessening his chances of living comfortably in the 'real world' – as if television represented reality.

The only words of sense in this grotesque debate came from Alan, who when asked how he would get his views on the outside life (if he were free and still not watching the box) replied, 'I would open my front door and look out at life.'

This nonsensical argument aside, the biggest shock of the hearing came by way of omission. Throughout the almost three-hour hearing, the words 'Strangeways' and 'riot' were not uttered once. But for the seriousness of the situation, it would have compared with the *Fawlty Towers* farce-line, 'Don't mention the war!' But this is no laughing matter. This is the matter of an unforgiving system, still bent on revenge, 16 years after it was exposed as rotten and brutal to the core.

Alan Lord is still in prison because of his part in the Strangeways uprising, yet the system that keeps him incarcerated dare not say as much. If it did then his supporters could point to masses of evidence, including Lord Justice Woolf's official inquiry report into the disturbance, to show that he and his fellow protesters were scapegoats for the failures of the prison service.

'The disturbances were planned as a limited protest, the majority of inmates shared the belief that conditions at the jail were unacceptable and inhumane... there are three requirements which must be met if the prison system is to be stable; they are security, control and justice... The April 1990 disturbances were a consequence of the failure of the prison system to conform to these basic rules.' (Woolf Report 1991).

So, officially, Alan Lord remains in prison due to fears that he is institutionalised! His good behaviour seemingly counts for little. The process is a sham and an affront to the justice that Woolf spoke about.

In his own words to the parole hearing: 'I behave, I do all the programmes, but the gate doesn't get any nearer.' A few days after the hearing Alan Lord received his answer. His application for Category D status was denied.

Those were the words of Eric Allison reporting in 2010. Eric followed my path through the system and also takes an interest in my life to this day.

I didn't expect to get the move to Category D because of refusing to take the courses they thought would help me progress – even though, for a number of years, I'd kept out of trouble and away from conflict with the screws. The only 'trouble' that comes to mind from my four years in Kingston almost took place when I was walking down the landing and met one of the screws.

'Lordy, I have to talk to you about your exercise,' he said to me.

'My exercise?'

He said he had a complaint from one of the other inmates about all the noise coming from my cell early in the morning.

'Hold on a minute, I'm very quiet with my workout in the morning and I've been doing the same routine for years. So if any inmate has got a problem with it, tell them to come to my cell. I don't complain about their loud music and shouting and carrying on late at night, and never have.'

The screw agreed with me.

'Right,' I said, 'from now on I'm not going to sneak around my cell trying to be as quiet as possible, I'm going to make as much noise as I want, just like they do, and let's see if the snake who is making the complaints comes forward!'

Surprise, surprise, no one ever did. I never got any complaints from the lads directly underneath me. In actual fact, they said they liked their morning call because it got them up early to do their studying.

I got on with my daily routine and kept to my own set of mates. I got visits with Joe and Dave from Liverpool, who always came no matter where I was placed in the country (if Everton wasn't playing that day, of course). They always made me laugh and lifted my spirits with their scouse humour. Joe had stood by me from day one; I was a young lad when I first went to prison and he was a father figure to me. I had a lot of respect and admiration for them both.

So I got on with it in Kingston, but felt like I'd been down a very long and bumpy road. I was getting older and things were starting to slow down for me, to get that little bit easier.

MOVING ON TO KINGSTON

I guess I'd just had enough of fighting the system.

But I did look forward to being free one day. I just had to hope I wasn't kept there because the regime thought I was institutionalised. That would be shameful.

CHAPTER TWENTY-SIX

REPATRIATION

Later that year a new governor came to Kingston. He was always approachable and I was always polite with him, giving him a nod whenever passing. I guess he could see from my behaviour that I was no trouble. I was called into the office one day for a board meeting and the new governor was sat there.

'Hello Alan, how are you?' he asked.

'I'm very well, thank you very much.'

'Take a seat. Can you tell me why you think you should get moved to a Category-C prison?'

'Due to the fact that, after all the years I've spent in various prisons,' I told him, 'my behaviour and my outlook have obviously changed.'

He agreed. 'You've been impeccable here, Alan, and you well deserve to go on a progressive move, so I'll be putting you down for Category C.'

So off I went back to my cell, with thoughts of the gates opening. I never thought I'd be this close to setting foot on the road to freedom – although, while I was in Kingston, I'd tried to get Belizean citizenship to see if I could get repatriated or deported to my father's homeland.

I got the idea from an Irish friend at the time who was applying for his Irish passport. He asked if I'd ever thought about getting a Belizean passport because it could lead me to freedom. I wrote off to the Belizean Embassy in London and they were very helpful in giving me information about births, deaths and marriages. I sent the money off that was requested and received a letter back saying they'd found my father's birth certificate. They sent me a copy of it and it was a surprise to actually find out who my grandparents were.

And I also received a letter from the UK Borders Agency, saying that they didn't object to me going to Belize and even offering to pay my fare, sending directions and a map of Belmopan, the capital city. I said I'd pay my own way and thanked them for their help.

My intention was to start a new life there, but once the parole board got wind they put a stop to it right away. They said that not only was I a life-sentence prisoner but also a risk to members of the public, not only here but in other countries.

These feeble claims came from the parole board, police, Home Office and prison authorities, but they were nothing but empty rhetoric. Despite my two previous escapes, in 1990 and 1993, while unlawfully at large I did not commit any crimes. Upon my eventual release, the court, the police and the judge all accepted that fact. It was noted by Mr Sturgeon, an official assigned to the Category-A department within the prison service headquarters, in his shorthand notes that, as far as he was concerned and from the evidence scrutinised, 'Lord posed no risk to members of the general public.'

I'd been in prison for twenty-six years and had served the time for the crime I was originally sentenced for, but that didn't count. I was not involved in any violent act whilst in Strangeways Prison during the protest in 1990. And I just couldn't understand why they wanted to keep me locked up in the United Kingdom when another country – the country of my father's origin – was willing to take me in. It made no sense whatsoever to me.

I gave up trying in the end because it seemed that, no matter what I did, I always hit a brick wall. I was even going to employ a Belizean solicitor to stand for me but felt by then it'd have been a waste of time and money.

Plus I knew the Home Office didn't give a shit about the safety of their citizens, especially when they let migrants in who'd committed serious crimes in their own country, including murder. I'd become quite cognisant of the law governing the removal of foreign nationals and it clearly stated the following: if you are a habitual criminal, have no allegiance to Queen and Country, and are considered a threat to the public, then all of these predispose towards deportation or repatriation. It so happened that during this period another life-sentence prisoner was due to be released from a Category-D open prison to return to his family in London. He'd lived in the UK from a very young age, but the Home Secretary asked for his deportation to Sicily as he was seen as a threat under the very same law I was seeking to apply to myself.

He later went on to the European Courts of Human Rights and won his right to remain in the country. I was left with no alternative but to wait, but no matter when I was to be released, I'd still try and get a Belizean passport. Maybe one day I'd go and live in Belize; I had no one on the out and, if I wanted to, I could start a new life there. I'd always felt a connection with Belize, and I wanted to try to move on and forget about the nightmare I'd been through.

But at the same time I couldn't help thinking about how hypocritical the whole system was. I will remain on a life licence till the day I die, with some variation in restrictions, yet once a foreign national on a life licence is deported it's no longer applicable.

I was disappointed, but I could see some light at the end of the tunnel. I was getting responses from 10 Downing Street, the Secretary of State and the Queen's Office. It was funny to see the screws' faces when my official letters were privately delivered to me. I was soon sent to attend my second parole board hearing; they were already aware of me getting my Category-C.

I'd read up on parole board hearings and learned I could tape the hearing for my reference. I don't think they were very happy with my request but, knowing I'd read up on my rights, the judge agreed I could record it on the equipment they had in there.

I'd had my suspicions and came to the hearing equipped with a twelve-hour tape recorder borrowed off my mate

Malcolm. Just before the hearing, a security officer turned on the tape. A couple of minutes later it made a funny noise and stopped.

'I think the tape is broken, Your Honour,' the security officer said to the judge.

The judge said we'd just have to carry on, but I stood up and said, 'It's alright, Your Honour, I've brought my own tape!'

You should have seen their faces. I don't think the judge liked me very much; he didn't look at me once, there was no eye contact at all.

After that day I advised every inmate up for parole to take a tape in with them, especially lifers. It kind of freaks the authorities out because they can't mess up. They have to talk to the prisoners in a manner they do not normally practise off-tape.

I'd eventually got my Category-C, and one of the lifer team came to see me. Her name was Tracey Mundy, and whenever I sent any correspondence to the team I addressed them to Tracey & Tracey Co, because their names were Tracey Mundy and Tracey Gamblin. They were very helpful, unbiased and understanding of my plight.

Tracey advised me to go to HMP Buckley Hall in Rochdale, because she said Risley Prison had quite a lot of screws from Manchester, who still held grudges and might conduct vendettas against me. I thanked her for her advice and she put me down for a move.

I had a night stop at Winchester in a single cell with no problems, but when we stopped off the day after at Rye Hill Prison, they tried to double me up. I wasn't having it;

LIFE IN STRANGEWAYS

I waited in the reception area for quite a while until, in the end, they threw me in a cell meant for two – though I went in alone. It was disgusting; so bad that I ended up standing up all night in the middle of the cell.

CHAPTER TWENTY-SEVEN

BITING
THE BULLET

I arrived at HMP Buckley Hall after travelling for two days. I was glad to get out of the shithole I'd just come from and to get my cell sorted out. I couldn't wait to bleach it out, get cleaned up and get my head down. I hadn't slept properly for two nights.

Buckley Hall was a Category-C prison; throughout the years it had changed from a male prison to a female prison and then back to a male prison again. It had also changed hands from the private sector to a public sector prison and then back to private. I'm in favour of the private sector because of the better conditions and treatment. Buckley Hall was also very scenic, it was on a hill and there was nothing but fields around for miles. I could see the hillside from my cell window.

I was placed on the induction wing at first, which wasn't bad, though the first morning didn't start very well. I was on the phone to my friend Joe to let him know where I'd been moved to when a female screw shouted at me to put the phone down. I just ignored her.

When I'd finished talking to Joe I walked back to my cell and there were two female screws stood in a dogmatic stance, glaring at me.

'Why were you on the phone, lad?' one of them asked me.

'I didn't know I wasn't allowed to use the phone,' I said. 'It doesn't state anywhere on the walls that there are time restrictions.'

I also told them I didn't appreciate their talking down to me. They looked surprised at my outspokenness, but I spoke in a polite manner. When I explained that I'd only just arrived at Buckley Hall, which they should have been aware of, they were alright with me. They told me to follow the basic rules so we'd get on without any further problems. I just went back to my cell and banged up.

After I finished my induction I was sent for a check-up with the doctor and to see the chaplaincy – although I told the chaplain I was a non-believer, even though my parents were Christians. I asked him how he expected me to have any kind of faith after what I was put through, especially since the chaplain at Strangeways Prison told my trial that he'd witnessed me walking down the middle of the chapel brandishing two sticks, which never happened. There were nineteen screws in attendance on the day of the protest, and none mentioned in their statements that they'd seen me with sticks anywhere; the chaplain was the only one.

The chaplain in Kingston didn't know what to say. I walked out and never attended chapel again. To me, priests are hypocrites and always have been throughout the centuries.

As part of your induction, you had to write down any educational and vocational skills. When I handed my paperwork in to the education officer she saw I had a degree and asked me how long it had taken. I'd gained a BA honours degree on an arts foundation course and did an Open University course in health and safety, but I found it odd because she should have known a prison degree would take six years.

I filled out a form to go onto the garden section, and a few days later received notification that I'd been accepted, which I was happy about. It meant I'd be outside all day, working with nature in the fresh air. I didn't think they'd give me a job outside, given my previous escapes, but I guess they knew that any further attempts would only send me backwards. They knew how hungry I was to be free.

Working on the gardens was good: it was relaxing and very therapeutic. I really enjoyed working with the tree plantations. The other lads who were working on the gardens had constructed a polytunnel behind C-wing; it was quite big and there were all kinds of vegetables and flowers growing in there. The lads were very proud of their plantations and protective of what they'd seeded.

It was July when I first started working on the gardens. As the weather was so nice I used to work outside in my shorts.

It gave me a spring in my step knowing that, once I'd got my circuit and weight training in, I was going outside in the gardens all day.

Then one day as I was going to work, there was a screw stood at the end of my wing looking at me funny. He was a nasty piece of work. As I walked past him he said in a very aggressive and dogmatic manner, 'You're not going out dressed like that!'

I'd been wearing my shorts for the past few weeks and none of the other screws had a problem with it.

'I've had permission,' I told him.

'I do *not* care who has given you permission to wear your shorts,' he said in an even louder voice, 'I am telling you now, you are *not* going out dressed like that!'

'You might be *asking* me not to go out in my shorts, but you are definitely not *telling* me,' I replied to him calmly.

'I am the senior officer today and I don't know who has been letting you wear what the hell you want, but I am telling you *now* that you cannot go out dressed like that.'

'Well, maybe you should go and see the senior officer who told me it was appropriate.'

I didn't want to get into confrontation with him, so I just gave him a look, walked back to my cell and got changed into my tracksuit. He stood and glared at me when I walked past him to go to work. This screw was a loudmouth who looked like he could do with a good wash. He was dirty looking and, as I understood it, not even his own colleagues liked him.

And I continued to wear my tracksuit bottoms from that

day on. I think he was just pissed off because one of my calves was bigger than his waist. I was aware that he was always staring at me whenever he was on my wing and I think he wanted some kind of altercation with me. But I wasn't falling for it, because rumours were going round that I wouldn't last in Category-C as I was some kind of hard man who could easily be wound up. I guess they got that one wrong.

The only way to get one back at them was to beat the regime at their own game. They wanted to keep me inside for the rest of my life and the only way out would be to change tactics. That was why I'd become a so-called model prisoner; that was why I ignored their daily abuse; that was why I was so polite and kept out of any kind of conflict. It took me a long time to realise that fighting the system inside was not going to work; by getting out I'd beat the system and come out the better man.

I'd come to Buckley Hall to do the victim awareness course. Even though it was taken in the prison chapel that I was reluctant to enter, it was part of my plan for getting out. I put in my application for the course with a female chaplain, but when I went to see her she told me the course and programme had been stopped. I was placed in a very difficult situation, because part and parcel of my progress was supposed to be that course.

At that time I had an internal probation officer who I couldn't get on with. I felt like she couldn't understand what it was like to be a prisoner and when she introduced herself to me I thought she looked at me like I was a piece of shit.

'Don't you think those letters you are writing could be offensive to someone?' she said to me.

'I don't know what you mean by offensive: they're well written, polite, pleasant, constructive and straight to the point of my enquiry or complaint.'

She said she'd heard I was making a nuisance of myself to those on the receiving end. I told her the letters I wrote were no different than I would have written on the out. Just because I was in prison didn't mean I didn't have the right to take up issues and complaints.

Then she advised me to stop writing about the way things were run in her prison – about the course work I was supposed to do to progress through the system, about the way some screws were giving me sly digs about my size, and about how I wasn't able to wear my shorts outside in the summer months – and to complain to her if I had a problem. I told her I needed to do the victim awareness course that had been stopped, but all she was bothered about was my writing letters to various offices.

From that day on I didn't want to speak to her. Some inmates would put up with the way they were penalised by certain probation officers who let their position go to their heads, but I was never going to let that happen to me. I knew my rights and wouldn't tolerate the bullshit they came out with.

It was shortly coming up to my life sentence plan board (LSPB) of principal officers and psychologists who assessed life prisoners' behaviour and progress. I'd applied to go to a Category-D prison. My new probation officer was very negative and said she doubted I'd get the move. I was well aware that my life sentence plan reports contained good reviews and no objections, but I didn't get the Category D move even though I'd done the programmes that were requested. Yet again the door was closed in my face.

I started looking up other prisons that did the victim awareness course. Risley Prison in Warrington ran the course, though I'd heard all sorts of things about Risley – some good and some bad. I wrote to Risley and got a letter back from the psychology department, who confirmed they were happy to accept me onto the course and for me to be transferred to their prison.

The course date started in late 2011. I wrote to Mr Nicolson in the lifers department about my lack of progress in Buckley Hall. I was accepted to go to Risley Prison and happy that I'd got the chance to do the course sooner rather than later. The only thing about going down the categories was the even greater lack of respect for prisoners as the regime became ever more dogmatic.

I'd served a long and tiresome stretch among prisoners in the Category Ds where there were more clowns than in Billy Smart's circus. I'd served four months in Buckley Hall but had no ROTL (release on temporary licence) even though other inmates were allowed to go out weekly or on weekends. I was always refused whenever I put my request in, but I was happy knowing I'd soon be moving into an open prison.

I had no problems in Buckley Hall but I always felt like I wasn't welcome there. No matter where I landed, I had to take a look from the screws or abuse because of my past and my part in the Strangeways Prison protest. I sometimes felt like I was a monkey locked behind bars in a zoo – in fact I was called 'Monkey Man' many times, but I guess it's something you get used to after years of racial abuse.

What's more I enjoyed the gardens at Buckley Hall too. I remember one day one of the screws came up to me – they called him Torsion, I guess it was because he looked like he was pumped up with steroids – to offer me a better position on the gardens as a 'red band', which meant I'd have more freedom around the gardens, and I could break and go to the gym whenever I wanted. It was a bit like being a prefect at school; you looked after the gardens and watched over other inmates for better privileges. I turned it down, of course; I had no intention of progressing through their system with treats for good behaviour. I liked my sunbathing and banter with the lads too much to walk around with a red band on my arm.

I also met a lad called Barry in Buckley Hall. I felt sorry for him, he seemed institutionalised, didn't want to do any courses and found it hard to get along. I had a good talk to him one day and told him it was the only way he was going to get out, but he didn't listen. Then he had an altercation with that screw Torsion; I heard it might have been a set-up but it resulted in Barry being set backwards to serve much more time. It made me realise I had to keep my head down because there was only one place I wanted to go.

And I also met Cliff, a nice guy from Newcastle who'd been in prison since he was a kid. He had his ups and downs but ended up being released in January 2013, which I was pleased about. I'd first met Cliff in Hull's segregation unit; he had mental health issues and suffered with mild schizophrenia, but he was alright. Then when I was in Buckley Hall, working, I heard someone shouting, 'Alan Lord! Alan Lord!' To my surprise it was Cliff; I was so happy for him that he was on his way out. We made arrangements to meet in the grounds, as you would to meet up with an old friend for a pint (or a cup of tea in my case, being teetotal).

I used to order a newspaper in Buckley Hall called *Fight Racism! Fight Imperialism!* It was a left-wing paper and a good way to get to know what was going on. I'd actually been reading it for over twenty years at various prisons. Then one day, while I was sat reading my paper, one of the screws walked past and said, 'What is that you're reading?'

When I told him, he said I couldn't read it because it was defined as communism.

'Who's being dictatorial now?' I asked him.

I also told him I had permission from the Home Office to read the paper. But he took it off me.

'Well, you've not had permission to read it in here.'

I just walked back to my cell and started writing a letter to the Home Office. The only way I knew how to get results now was to put pen to paper. I also phoned my solicitor, Nicki; she started laughing and said how pathetic it was. She told me to wait until they brought my paper back 'with a red face'. She was right; it wasn't long before it was brought back. It just proved to me how much each individual screw made up their own set of rules and regulations.

The day soon came to be transferred to Risley Prison. I had no problems with my transfer. The security officers from

Buckley Hall even had a bit of banter with me on the journey. They said Risley was looking forward to having Alan Lord in their prison, they wanted to study me – in other words, they wanted to meet the Alan Lord who had nearly beaten the system; to see what Alan Lord looked like after spending all those years in various prisons; to see the person that fought back against the regime; the person who was too defiant to come off the roof at Strangeways until he was captured after being led into false negotiations; who had escaped from a high-security police station and then again from Manchester Crown Court; who had given up his freedom so that fellow prisoners past and present would not have to go through the degrading daily slop-out, the minimal weekly showers and non-existent exercise time.

At the same time, I did look back over my life and think to myself, *What a journey!* There were times when I thought I'd never get through the time I was facing. I went in a young lad and had to grow up under the regime. I just had to take each day at a time. I learned that the best thing to do in such a bad situation is to read books, put pen to paper and educate myself, I just wish I'd had advice and support from my parents and an education out in the real world. Things might have been so different.

I'd also met some amazing people (inmates) along the way and some downright nasty scum (screws) who had it in for me from the start because I was a 'murdering black bastard'.

The only thing I didn't like was being scrutinised by other people. I didn't want to be any kind of prison legend. I just wanted to move on and start a new life. I'd been punished for my crime by having my liberty taken away from me, but I also stood up for my rights as a human being. I did not expect to be treated without humanity or to endure such a level of brutality, like I was an animal. I didn't hear the judge saying I'd be subject to racial and psychological abuse, kicked and punched around by the screws throughout my sentence. He didn't tell me I'd be starving some of the time because of the terrible food that was served and that I'd stink like a pig because I could only shower once a week; that I'd suffer fatigue because of lack of exercise in the fresh air. I never heard the judge reading out those particular punishments when he was sentencing me.

CHAPTER TWENTY-EIGHT

THE FINAL COURSE

I arrived at Risley and went to the reception area to get my things sorted out. I was put on the induction wing for one week. I did my health and safety and went to my cell to clean it and bleach it out, the same as always.

The next day a lady came down to see me about the CALM course; she told me it was starting within the next few days. I was looking forwards to getting started and was settling in, but there was a misunderstanding. The following day she came back down and told me she was very sorry, but I couldn't go on the course because I hadn't been risk assessed.

She said the parole board had told her I had to take a risk assessment course before I could do the CALM course. I was quite agitated and deep down inside I was fuming, as I didn't have a clue what the hell was going on and felt quite embarrassed in front of this lady who was trying to help me. I knew it wasn't her fault and told her I'd take it up with the right department.

So I wrote to the psychology department and found out I had to do the risk assessment course first. So I just had to wait and be patient. But I found this strange as I'd already been assessed as warranting the CALM course, and this had been endorsed by the parole board.

I was placed on the third landing and given a cleaning job, sweeping and mopping the landings and cleaning the showers and recess area. It wasn't that bad; at least I knew it'd be cleaned properly. I have a thing about cleanliness and bleached everywhere every day.

The gym was adjacent to E-wing, where my cell was; the laundry was also on my floor, which was good. I went to do some washing one day and asked this feller if he was working in the laundry. When he said yes I asked him for some powder to wash my clothes, but he said he was too busy when he clearly wasn't doing anything. I just walked back to my cell. If it had been a few years ago I'd probably have made him eat the powder, but I'd learnt to walk away.

Soon after, the same feller knocked on my door; he apologised for not giving me some soap powder and said he remembered me from Wakefield. He clearly didn't; I knew someone else had told him who I was. He said he'd take my clothes to the laundry and wash them for me. I said okay, thanks, and from that day on I had my clothes washed for me every day.

I also went to the gym every day and got into a routine. I didn't train at weekends because it was my rest time; I worked my body hard throughout the week. The only time I had anything approaching an argument was with one of the PEIs (physical education instructors). It was with regard to my neck exercises; she didn't approve and expressed concern that my neck could be seriously injured, or I could even break it. I looked at her in disbelief, explaining that I'd been doing my neck exercises for many years and never once had a PEI shown concern.

There was also a time in the gym when this toy gangster tried to get lippy with me; he knew my situation and that no matter what he said to me I couldn't do anything about it. If we were in a dispersal prison I'd have jumped all over him, but this time I had to bite my lip.

'Did you hear the way that prick just spoke to you, Al?' one of the lads said as we were walking back to the cells.

He asked me if I wanted him to go back to the gym and give him a good hiding, but I told him to leave it. I had to stay away from trouble as I didn't want anything getting in the way of my getting out. Then I found out the next day someone *had* given him a good hiding. I had to laugh to myself because I knew it was on my behalf; I just wished I'd have been a fly on his wall.

I did the risk assessment course and had the chance to do the CALM course. I enjoyed the role playing: finding out how far to push people before they were at breaking point; how long it would take someone to push me into reacting in a negative way. I also liked the victim awareness booklet, which I found interesting despite my objections to courses in the past.

And I completed all targets successfully and happily. I didn't think I'd enjoy the course and just wanted to get the paper, but it turned out to be very interesting. I still believe that courses will never change a person; you need to want to change for yourself.

I clearly remember bringing up the issue during a parole-board hearing, when I was asked by the judge for my view on courses.

'Do you want the truth or do you want the lies?' I asked him.

He requested the truth.

'From my observation of people participating in these courses, the majority only did them under coercion and it'd be fair to say that manipulation and deceptiveness played a large part in the undertaking.'

The judge thanked me for my honesty.

There were around ninety men on my wing; most of them were foreign nationals. The food was no good in Risley, it was tasteless, sloppy and the portions were not enough to feed a mouse. But I had an internal probation officer who was very understanding and professional towards me. Her name was Helen Marques, she was Brazilian and had been in the probation service for over twenty years. She was a very good listener.

I was eventually moved to the top wing in the corner cell, which was much better; it felt like I was on my own because I had no other cells facing me. I also met a lad from Manchester at that point who was also a lifer. He was alright, a bit of an odd character but he was harmless; he'd been involved in drugs, something I'd never had anything to do with. I stayed away from the drugs trade even though there was a hell of a lot of money to be made. Fitness and wellbeing remained my only fix.

And I liked the gym in Risley Prison; I could get a good workout with the weights. I also passed the time writing and even had a word processor sent in there. I was able to get on with my paperwork and really enjoyed the change from handwriting to using the processor. Until one day when I was working out in the gym, that is.

Two officers came over and told me they'd done a cell search and taken my word processor out. They told me a female officer had told them I could be breaching security regulations.

'You could be counterfeiting visiting slips,' they said.

I couldn't believe what I was hearing, especially as my visits were very rare. I ended up having my processor sent out to my mate Joe. I wasn't going to let them think they had one over on me by taking my property and keeping it in their prison.

Then I went to see the senior screw but he couldn't do anything about it. He told me the female screw who ordered my processor to be taken out was a bitch who no one liked and she was out of order for what she'd done.

'All she's done is make me write even more letters, only this time I'll be writing with a pen, not a machine,' I told him. 'Tell her not to worry about my processor because I'm not going anywhere and I have all the time in the world to write as many letters as I want.'

She obviously didn't know the difference between a word processor and a computer. But she couldn't stop me from writing letters, which is all a word processor does.

I used to go to the library once a week to read about other countries, the unknown, outer space and UFOs. I read about Belize, where my father was born, and tried to trace some family history but it wasn't easy as resources were limited.

Then I had a board meeting in Risley about being down-graded to a Category-D prison and was given the go-ahead to apply, because I'd completed both the risk assessment and CALM courses. I'd also kept myself out of trouble.

After a few days of waiting I was told that the parole board accepted the recommendation for me to be downgraded and I was going to be moved to a Category-D prison shortly. I was over the moon about that, because the next step from Category-D was home.

And I knew deep down I was going to get it because I'd done everything the last parole board had put in front of me. But I tried not to let my imagination run away because things had gone wrong for me in the past.

I was in my cell one day, sorting my things out, and they came to take me to another prison. I did not know where I was going to till I got to the reception area, but when I was signing out I was told it was Sudbury Prison in Derbyshire. I was happy with that because it was a northern prison. Another step closer to home.

CHAPTER TWENTY-NINE

THE LAST STANCE

I arrived at HMP Sudbury and felt good. I felt a sense of achievement. I'd come a long way and felt like this could be my last stance. Sudbury is an open prison and doesn't have a high level of security. No dogs or secure fences. No outside locks on the doors. It is a prison system that trusts the inmates not to abscond, which was a first for me. It took some time to get used to, because I was always looking for a way out and there it was – right in front of my nose. But I dared not think of going anywhere because I was so close to getting out 'the right way'.

Sudbury had one policy that I just couldn't tolerate, which was that I had to double up in a cell (or room). My objection to this was that I don't smoke or watch television or listen to the radio; I didn't want to be awake at all hours making conversation with a complete stranger; I'd spent the past thirty-one years in a cell on my own. The other thing I didn't like about Sudbury was that everything was communal. There was also no soundproofing in the walls, and the young lads had their music blasting most nights until the early hours of the morning. This created a head-on conflict for me, but after much deliberation I was able to have a single room.

A percentage of the lads were allowed to go outside the prison to do various jobs in the community, either paid or voluntary. They could also work inside the prison. We were allowed to walk round the fields at Sudbury and were trusted to adhere to the rules, which were minimal compared to what I was used to. It felt like the closest thing that I'd experienced to freedom since my last escape, over twenty-one years ago.

Sudbury was an old American army base, which housed injured soldiers in the Second World War. It was set out just like you would imagine it to be and it wasn't too far away from Sudbury village, where most of the prisoners worked. It was very relaxed at Sudbury but sometimes you got screws walking round the village, to make sure no one was smoking drugs or sitting around in pubs.

Sudbury Prison was my last stop before freedom, so I didn't want to mess things up in any way, shape or form. I didn't know how long I was going to be in there and had no idea of my next parole date. All I had to focus on was getting through each and every day, knowing that very soon I'd have the gates open for me – even though I knew full well I'd never be a free man as such, because I'd come out with a life licence and didn't know what my restrictions would be.

I was in Sudbury for around eighteen months but had to

do a lay down for around four months, while I was assessed and prepared for life on the outside. That meant no ROTL (Release on Temporary Licence), which was a bit annoying because when the lads were going out for their weekend ROTLs I had to watch them go past. Most of the time I was in the fields, just walking around.

While in Sudbury there was one event I wasn't very happy about. A local newspaper printed an article about me, saying: 'Alan Lord, a convicted murderer and Strangeways Prison ringleader, is now in Sudbury Prison.' I really thought it would mess things up for my release. But the governor had a chat with me about my concerns and reassured me it would cast no shadow on my progress. He told me the parole-board meeting would only take into consideration how I was conducting myself here and now. He told me I had nothing to worry about and to just carry on with what I was doing.

I felt better after hearing that, although it was hard living amongst the filth inside Sudbury Prison. The young inmates who were only there for weeks, or sometimes months, were dirty, untidy little shits. I was beginning to think they just wanted to get away from their girlfriends and kids for a short break, or catch up with their mates who were serving longer sentences. I also met up with a few lads from other prisons who knew what real prison time was like. I used to look at some of the kids in there and realise they didn't know what it was like in a hardcore prison. They didn't want to end up where I'd been.

Having progressed through the categories, from the

dispersal system to categories C and D, the immaturity of plastic gangsters sometimes pissed me off immensely. But remaining calm was a priority for me. It was quite difficult at times and their behaviour only served to underline the screws' preconceptions, as they probably perceived all prisoners as having the same mentality. I wanted so much to tell them about the opportunity they had to turn their lives around before it was too late, but most of the time they were just too immature to even bother with.

I found employment in the kitchen, which was good. Even though I'd worked in a kitchen before I'd never worked on the server, because I wouldn't want to dish out the pitiful quantities of food. It was different in Sudbury because there was plenty of food to go round.

Plus I could also cook my own food, so it had its benefits. It was a very busy, bustling atmosphere. I took advantage obviously; I never went hungry and I was moved from vegetable preparation to the storeroom. That was a trustee job, which was good to have on your CV for the parole board.

It was an Aladdin's cave for me in stock control; I wasn't going to be a pushover when some of the little gangsters tried to put their orders in. I'd only oblige if there was a deal to be done. There was a lot of wheeling and dealing going on in Sudbury. I suppose it passed the time and brought a bit of excitement to the camp, and it gave me something to look forward to each day.

I soon got back into my routine of weight training and early morning circuit sessions, and in the kitchen I got my daily requirement of food. I was also moved to a better part of the prison; it was quieter so I could get some much-needed sleep. I could at last settle down in my newly bleached room that took most of the afternoon to clean from top to bottom, due to the dirty tramp that was in there before. But once it was cleaned it was a different place.

So I carried on writing and working in the kitchen, and my days were pretty full. I'm not saying it was a holiday camp or a walk in the park, but I had to make the best of a bad situation, At the end of the day I was still in prison and I was still haunted by the past, especially when it was brought to everyone's attention by the media. I was still headline news in local papers more than thirty years after my original sentencing, as if serving that length of time wasn't enough. I'd gone into prison as a boy and expected to be heading out in my fifties.

I met up with some old acquaintances in Sudbury from my periods in various prisons throughout the years, but spent most of the time on my own. I guess I was old school to some inmates as the time I'd served was more than a lifetime. I also had respect from most I met along the way because of my part in the Strangeways Prison protest and standing up for prisoners' rights.

One of the lads in Sudbury was working as a delivery driver and needed me to wake him up early in the mornings. I was up at four to do my circuit training and it was funny, because I used to knock on his door with my torch and shine it in his face like the Gestapo.

'Come on, feller, up!' I would call to him.

I just tried to get through the days and keep busy; knowing

I was so close to being released was sometimes like walking on eggshells. The only thing I didn't like at Sudbury was the lack of hygiene; it was a shameful place when it came to showering and keeping clean. I am a very clean man, and for the first time in all the years of my imprisonment I had to share the recess with dirty little pigs; the toilets were always full of shit marks and the showers constantly full of scum. I had to keep using bleach everywhere I went.

In truth, I couldn't wait to get out of that shithole. I also had a problem living alongside young inmates doing short stints; they were the ones that were blasting the music at all hours. I sometimes had to go and have words and tell them to have some respect for others wanting to sleep. I was sometimes ignored and had to bite my tongue, especially when some of them were being a bit lippy. I didn't want to lose it and end up on a report. I needed to keep a clean slate.

I liked working in the stores and being trusted – even though I used to sort a couple of the lads out with some goodies. I know it wasn't mine to give, but as long as I was careful we all stayed happy and well fed. I did have to duck and dive a few times, but it was worth it to have some dairy goodies at the end of the day.

What's more I always took every opportunity to get out and walk round the grounds, even in the cold winter when the dark nights would draw in. I found a place away from everyone and used to sit there looking up at the stars in wonderment for hours. On two occasions I actually saw shooting stars go right across the sky. It was fantastic to see.

I felt at peace out in the fields. I also loved to be outside in the summer months, listening to the birds and catching the sun's rays. It was at those times that I felt I'd missed out on my life. I'd missed out on so many things that I could have done.

The first time I got out of Sudbury, I went escorted by an officer and another lifer called Mark to Derby town centre. I needed to go to the public toilets at the bottom of some steps, and whilst descending to the loo I lost my footing and slid down a few steps on my arse. Mark laughed his head off and so did I – but at the same time I felt like a right dick. It'll come across as absurd but you become accustomed to prison's interior infrastructure. The prison steps were quite big and wide, and the public toilet steps, where I went flying, were very narrow.

I was given £50 that I could spend on whatever I wanted, but I had to spend it all. I also had £100 of my own money when I went out on my first ROTL. My wages were £14 each week and I spent it on extra food and chocolate.

We had a walk around the town centre and I bought a few provisions and some clothes. I found it very strange to be walking around the shops; it was very bright and noisy, and the traffic was mad. I was surprised to see just how much there was on the roads and I was a little bit nervous crossing them. I felt like I'd just landed from outer space. The cars were very fast and it was very strange to see people's faces – especially children's faces.

I applied to go out on my own and was granted two weekend outings. I also went out with my mate Ashey and then it got to my monthly ROTLs, when I went home at weekends. I remember going to see my sister for the first time; I just knocked on her door and she couldn't believe it when I was stood there. I also got to see my nieces and nephew, whom I hadn't seen for years.

One time, when I went out walking in the grounds of Sudbury Prison, a cat started following me. I stopped and stroked it and it followed me back to the prison. I kept it in the chapel, away from the other inmates at first, and started feeding it with tins of tuna. I made a bed up for it and even Felix the cartoon cat would have been envious of our prison cat. Some of the other lads also started to spoil it and got used to having the cat around – until one day a woman came and said the cat was hers and she wanted it back. She took the cat and didn't even thank us for looking after it. The cat had been free to go whenever it wanted but never strayed from the prison, because it was well fed and got lots of attention. But the woman took it back and that was the end of that.

It was good to get out of Sudbury at weekends, but in winter it was sometimes hard to get back in time because of the thick snow. I always went out with Ashey and Mark. I knew it'd not be long before I was up in front of the parole board and I had a feeling I'd be released. But I also had doubts in the back of my mind; the thought of being free after all those years confined in various prisons was very exciting, but also a little bit daunting at the same time.

The day soon came round for my parole-board meeting; I was only in for half an hour. It was the shortest hearing I'd ever had. A QC called Flo Klause represented me; she was a character of tremendous vibrancy and moral strength who spoke for lifers at parole-board hearings. It'd be fair to say that many authoritarian figures trembled at the thought of Flo being in attendance. I was very grateful to her; because of her presence I was granted my parole. I was going to be free at last.

Even though I was so excited that it was finally over and the time had come to go home, I felt I couldn't tell anyone the good news of my release. I didn't want to rub it in anyone's face, because there were some lads who were probably going to be in there for quite some time. I had to keep it to myself and wait for the official letter and my release date. Then I could do the right thing and let the lads know just before I left.

CHAPTER THIRTY

ROAD TO REDEMPTION

I got my release letter not long after the parole-board meeting. I went through the process of being discharged and sorting my belongings out, and I was also appointed a new probation officer. When I finally got my date I couldn't wait for it to come round. It was 3 December 2012: a day I'll never forget.

All sorts of things were running through my head. I went to see a couple of the lads before I got my head down on the night before my release. I explained that I'd known for a while but didn't want to say anything because they were staying behind. They understood and were happy for me.

I got up very early on my last day of imprisonment; in fact I don't think I slept a wink all that night. My last night was very long.

After having breakfast, I walked to the reception with a feeling of excitement at my last checkout. It seemed fantastic that, for the first time in thirty-two years, I was checking out to go home, not to be transferred to another prison.

Next I was escorted to the door with my paperwork and a small bag, with £46 in my pocket. I got to the gatehouse and had a last bit of banter with the officers; I felt over the moon as I walked out.

I was released with two other lads and one of them gave me a lift to the station, where I got a train to Liverpool. I had to stay at a hostel on Aigburth Street for one month before I could move on, into another world. Another chapter of my life was about to start but it was all a bit daunting, to say the least.

The thing is I have always felt like people have mis-understood me, and maybe felt intimidated by my size, the colour of my skin or the deep tone of my voice. I just hoped people on the out would give me a chance, because deep down I'm nothing like how the police and the press have portrayed me. I think that people who truly know me would say I'm a considerate person who would do anything for anyone.

Even though I'm now free from prison, I'll never be free from the terrible memories of the past thirty-two years. It was never my intention to take David Gilbert's life and I'm truly sorry for his family's loss. I'll never forget that day for the rest of my life. I've done the time for the crime, and know there are many people who'd have liked to see me locked away forever. But I also know there are many folk who think my punishment was too harsh, considering my age and the circumstances surrounding the crime.

I cannot help thinking that if capital punishment was still in place, I wouldn't be here. I'd have been hanged many years ago. Nor would I have exposed the prison system, for which a further ten years of my life was unjustly taken. I was very young and naive when I was convicted of murder; I've now spent thirty-two years in various prisons and hope I can be forgiven for the crime I was sentenced for. I also hope that I'm one of those people who do genuinely deserve a second chance.

Not that I'm ever going to be a completely free man because I'm on a life licence. I walk around sometimes, looking over my shoulder in case anyone tries to stitch me up. Because I know there are people on the out who'd resent the fact that I'm getting on with my life – especially some of the old screws from the prison system.

I don't know where I'm going or where I'll end up, but I'll do my utmost to avoid any kind of confrontation that could lead me back inside. I'll always walk away from trouble and will make the most of every day.

I'll always be thankful that I've been given the chance of a fresh start in life. I'll be able to do the things I've never done before, like getting on a tram in Manchester; looking out of the window on a train while travelling through the countryside; looking at the animals in the fields. Just going out to see the shopping centres that look so futuristic and the new buildings in the city centre is wonderful to me. I'm now able to do the simplest things that many people take for granted, but which I haven't been able to do for the past thirty-two years.

I can now move on and try to find some kind of peace and happiness with what time I have left. But I'll never be a free man. I will always be under the scrutiny of the authorities till the day I die.

CHAPTER THIRTY-ONE

TWO YEARS ON...

It hardly feels like two years ago since I walked through the prison gates. It's gone so fast; I've been busy with the book and setting up my own weightlifting gym in Radcliffe, Greater Manchester. I wanted to put something back into the community, to help the teenagers get into fitness instead of hanging around the streets, getting into all kinds of trouble. I've been there and I know how easy it is to take the wrong path.

At the same time I wanted to carry on with my own weights regime, so having my own gym worked not only for me but for people who were looking for old-school training. I did try and find employment, but who would employ me? Not only did I have a thirty-two-year prison sentence hanging over my head but there was also my age, and my lack of experience in the real world.

As you know from reading this book, I've always been dedicated to my weight training and circuit training. But I never thought for one minute I'd be able to open my own gym, as much as I'd have loved to.

Then one day at the Job Club, I spoke to an adviser who told me about the loans Business Solutions were giving to people like me to help them get into self-employment. I was with Anita at the time and she encouraged me to go for it. So I applied for a business loan, but at first they knocked me back. However, with the help and determination of Anita, and the business plan that she created for me, I was able to buy the equipment I needed and opened my place in July 2014: AL's Gym.

Since opening the gym I've met some fantastic people who don't frown on me for my past. I've been able to get the teenagers into the gym and see them stick with it all through the summer holidays. To my surprise, they keep coming back. I give them advice, help them with circuit training and talk to them about the dangers of taking steroids, and the harm it can do to their bodies.

I'm taking each and every day one step at a time, building my business and rebuilding my life. I don't take anything for granted. I'm grateful for the second chance in life that I've been given.

AFTERWORD

I started writing Alan Lord's memoir because I believed his life sentence was questionable, and his confession to murder (as opposed to manslaughter) under duress unjust. I also believed in Alan's personal campaign for the human rights and dignity of prisoners, from lifers to those serving time for petty crime (though he had no sympathy for child abusers or sex offenders under any circumstances).

Throughout my experience of writing this book, I've had nothing but admiration for Alan's endless fight against injustice and the inhumane treatment of prisoners. I also had a strange feeling that I was writing this book about the life of someone other than Alan Lord, because the person in this book and the person I've spent the past six months with seem to be two different people.

Alan does not have the slightest iota of aggression in his

body. I've never met such a placid, patient and compassionate person. He speaks with clarity and possesses a fine intellect. It was his compassion that led him to rebel against the regime while incarcerated, enabling him to stand up and fight for what he believed in, no matter what.

Alan Lord's persistent fight for prisoners' rights and his part in the HMP Strangeways riot led to the abolishment of the degrading slop-out, and the extension of what were once weekly showers. There were also changes in how prisoners were expected to be locked up in overcrowded cells for twenty-three out of twenty-four hours each day and could only have one change of clothes each week.

Alan is not saying that prisoners should live in a holiday camp, merely that they are in prison and are punished by having their liberty taken away from them. Prisoners should not suffer years of physical and mental abuse behind locked doors.

Writing this book has sometimes been an emotional journey, especially while researching the crime itself. I remember looking through coverage in the *Manchester Evening News*, at the library. It had been front-page news then, with the headline 'Manhunt For Killer In Crumpsall'. On that front page was a photo of David Gilbert, the man Alan was charged with murdering. I looked at the reaction on his face and could clearly see it etched in pain and remorse. Alan went very silent and withdrew after only working on the research for half an hour. I too had to stop. I knew it was bringing everything back to him and it was just too much to take in.

AFTERWORD

Alan told me it was the first time he had seen a picture of Mr Gilbert, and it was a shock to see a photo of the man whose life he had unintentionally taken. Even though it was over thirty-two years ago, the pain and guilt were showing through his eyes and in his voice. We ended the research session for that day and Alan didn't speak one word all the way back to the tram station.

I was intrigued by the determination of his will to survive and beat the system. I've also been shocked at the level of brutality Alan endured throughout his imprisonment and his bitter revenge in fighting back. But he stood up against the regime because he did not want them to break him. He was labelled violent and dangerous, but they wanted to portray him like that so they could constantly lock him up in the segregation unit.

Alan has made it through the past thirty-two years and has definitely come out a better person. I do hope he enjoys his freedom, although it comes with a life licence attached. I wish him well in all he does in the future.

Anita Armstrong